Ethnologia Europaea

Journal of European Ethnology

Volume 47:1
2017

Special issue:

50 Years of Ethnologia Europaea – Readers' Choices from Half a Century

MUSEUM TUSCULANUM PRESS

Printed in Sweden by Exakta, Malmö 2017
Cover and layout Pernille Sys Hansen, Damp Design
Cover photo Peter Nørby: *Allegory of Europe* by Nicolai Abildgaard, The Royal Danish Collection, Amalienborg
ISBN 978 87 635 4558 7
ISSN 0425 4597

This journal is published with the support of the Nordic Board for Periodicals in the Humanities and Social Sciences.

Ethnologia Europaea is an official journal of Société Internationale d'Ethnologie et de Folklore (SIEF).

sief

Museum Tusculanum Press
Dantes Plads 1
DK-1556 Copenhagen V
Denmark
www.mtp.dk

CONTENTS

50 YEARS OF *ETHNOLOGIA EUROPAEA*
Readers' Choices from Half a Century

Marie Sandberg and Monique Scheer, editors of Ethnologia Europaea

Editorial

Awards for movies and TV shows are called "Critics' Choice" and "People's Choice"; even a famous instant coffee brand is called "Taster's Choice". When one considers the extent to which the notion of "choice" is instrumentalized for the purposes not only of marketing products but also producing the illusion of a democratic process (voting for "the best"), it might seem odd that *Ethnologia Europaea* has picked up on this idea for its anniversary edition. But as we pondered the various formats with which we could adequately commemorate the 50th year of the publishing of the journal's very first volume in 1967, the other options seemed equally embedded in (neo)liberal ideologies, particularly of meritocracy, that is, ranking and competition. It is a rather common practice to provide an overview or retrospective of an artist's work by publishing a "best of" anthology (certainly the recent awarding of the Nobel Prize to Bob Dylan will be generating a number of these). But what does this title "best of" actually reflect? Who decides which works are the "best" ones? Would they have to be the "best" in terms of artistic quality, in terms of popularity, in terms of representativity?

Even the daunting task of picking from the opus of a single artist appears rather simple compared to compiling a "best of" from a whole community of scholars. How could we possibly choose the "best of" 50 years of *Ethnologia Europaea*, what would be the criteria? As the last few decades have seen a dramatic increase in pressure for scholars in the humanities to submit to the same kinds of evaluation mechanisms that were developed for the natural sciences, it would seem quite inappropriate to present a compendium of articles with the highest "impact factor" or number of citations according to Google scholar. In our rather small fields in particular, we know all too well how inaccurate and irrelevant these measurements can be. But it is all around us. In the digital age, ranking and rating has become a participatory activity all over the social media and on shopping platforms. The various forms of "liking" and "reviewing" seem to democratize the decision-making around quality – but also increase our sense that the whole process of ranking is somehow deeply flawed.

However, compiling a "best of" collection is not only an exercise in marketing, but also an everyday practice. The young bachelor in Nick Hornby's novel *High Fidelity* just cannot stop making Top-5 lists; being obsessed with choosing which should go first among his favourite rock-bands, movie-screens, or guitar-solos, his whole life turns into an enumerated assessment, including his ex-girlfriends. Perhaps in less fanatic ways, "best of" lists are also linked to personal commemorations, where the payback is merely the enjoyment of looking back and immersing oneself in the sense of how much time has passed. Every scrapbook, every photo album represents a kind of selection of highlights one wants to remember. Playlists, and in previous generations mixed tapes, might also serve this purpose, especially when prepared for someone as a gift: our favourite songs, the best ones from our youth, the best ones from our favourite band. Some of these are also uploaded to social media, blurring the lines between "participatory marketing" and simple sharing of personal favourites. But this practice does make clear that there is a great deal of pleasure to be derived from reviewing someone's selection of funniest TV-show punch lines, cutest kitten antics, or soccer goals.

Clearly, this is the effect we are aiming for by presenting a collection of articles from over the last 50 years of this journal: a celebratory retrospective. Beginning with the first issue from 1967, we sought to represent each decade, spreading the five articles out over the whole time period of publication. Our method of selection was, however, not based on any sort of quantitative ranking but – perhaps in accordance with the methodology of our disciplines – in asking some of our regular readers to pick an article they found particularly appealing. Their reasons for doing so are outlined in the comments accompanying each article. By this process we are hoping to remind present and future *Ethnologia Europaea* readers not only of some really great articles in past issues but also to allow some reflection on the continuities and changes within our field over these 50 years. The "reader's choice" collection is something in between a retrospective "best of" anthology and a *Reader's Digest*. But instead of presenting only excerpts of articles – and far from drawing on the white American middle-class Cold War culture that this magazine represented for decades – our idea was that the readers "digest" the articles they selected by discussing their choices from a personal as well as a scholarly point of view.

We also thought that the 50th birthday of *Ethnologia Europaea* would present a nice occasion for two of the previous editors, who each put their mark on the journal for several years, to look back at its journey. In his afterword, Orvar Löfgren thinks about how *Ethnologia Europaea* has reflected processes of inventing and re-inventing Europe, perhaps now even de-constructing it. The ways that *Ethnologia Europaea* participates are reflected in our choice of cover illustration: a "remake" of the original illustration that graced so many volumes in the past, *Allegory of Europe* by the Danish artist Nicolai Abildgaard (1743–1809).

The celebratory retrospective is, inevitably, also a view into the future. The comments on the articles show this well, and highlight the temporal experiences and perceptions of this undertaking. Löfgren makes use of *Ethnologia Europaea* as a time machine; one can go back and forth in time by diving into past volumes and papers of the journal, and Regina F. Bendix declares the journal to be taking an opposite course to aging, since it seems to grow younger every year. We very much like the idea of *Ethnologia Europaea* as a healthily aging spaceship warp-speeding our field into promising futures.

Here's to another 50 years!

TWO WAYS TO SHAPE A DISCIPLINE IN AN "EXTREMELY SUNDERED PART OF THE WORLD"

Sigurd Erixon and Alberto Cirese Inaugurate *Ethnologia Europaea*

Dorothy Noyes, The Ohio State University

An American folklorist reading the first issue of *Ethnologia Europaea* finds it natural to draw a trans-Atlantic comparison. In 1971, the long-established *Journal of American Folklore* published a special issue, "Toward New Perspectives in Folklore."[1] This collection of articles marked a social and intellectual watershed in U.S. folklore studies: influence shifted to a new generation of researchers and to the emerging paradigm of "verbal art as performance" within a larger ethnography of communication. The immediate "new perspectives" were heterogeneous, however, drawing on a range of disciplines and theories for inspiration. In part this resulted from the different backgrounds and empirical foci of the contributors; in part it was a sending out of trial balloons to see which might float. The common impulse was to build a science from the precarious institutional base of a field generally considered to be residual.

Sigurd Erixon's initiation of *Ethnologia Europaea* came four years earlier, in 1967. Having broken from SIEF, the International Society for Ethnology and Folklore, in the wake of a takeover by a faction of conservative folklorists (Rogan 2008), Erixon was making the last of a career-long series of efforts to craft a unified framework from a heterogeneous array of intellectual projects in Europe. The first volumes of the new journal consist largely of programmatic statements and stocktakings of the state of the field(s). Like their U.S. counterparts, the contributors were concerned with both institutional cohesion and intellectual coherence, and sought scientific foundations as the guarantor of both. Likewise, the Europeans too sought to redefine the disciplinary subject as contemporary or at least continuous, integral rather than residual to modernity (cf. Kirshenblatt-Gimblett 1998).

The Europeans were necessarily more aware than the Americans of institutional challenges and historical constraints. In the United States, "young Turks"[2] such as Alan Dundes, Dan Ben-Amos, Roger D. Abrahams, and Richard Bauman sought to cast off the baggage of disciplinary history and subdue their institutional tyrants in the process. In contrast, Géza de Rohan-Csermak, the first editor of *Ethnologia Europaea*, was at 41 the youngest contributor to the first issue. Everyone participating had been affected by one and in some cases two world wars. Their concern was not with creative destruction but with the restoration and renewal of cooperative scholarly projects insofar as that might be possible. Erixon writes of Europe as "an extremely sundered part of the world" (1967: 5). Although he refers immediately to the scarcity of survivals marking Europe's connections to regions usually studied by anthropologists, the phrase admits of many other readings.

Dorothy Noyes 2017: Two Ways to Shape a Discipline in an "Extremely Sundered Part of the World": Sigurd Erixon and Alberto Cirese Inaugurate *Ethnologia Europaea*.
Ethnologia Europaea 47:1, 7–10. © Museum Tusculanum Press.

Erixon's opening statement is a plea for cooperation. Ethnological activities are inevitably diverse, he maintains, given the "vast" scope of the field itself: that is, the vast range of social and cultural phenomena addressed by ethnologists. In the second half of the article he will endeavor to subdue that empirical panorama into order, but the diversity of scholarly practice is his real concern. Explicitly he speaks of national and regional variety, and by extension methodological and institutional differences, spread across university disciplines, museums, and archives of various kinds. Ideological diversity, clearly important both to East–West interaction and within Europe itself, is not mentioned, and neither – in 1967! – is inter-generational tension. The first elision, at least, is surely a tactical avoidance. Marxist perspectives from both sides of the Iron Curtain are in fact present in the first issue among other less apparent commitments; the political situation permitted careful relations with Eastern European scholars and a deeper interaction with the non-aligned Yugoslavians. Soon some cautious father-slaying was also evident: Hermann Bausinger's contribution to the memorial issue for Erixon tactfully challenged not the journal's own establishment but the *Theoriefeindlichkeit* of the folklorists from whom Erixon had detached himself (1968–69).

Bjarne Rogan's careful research (2008 and elsewhere) has elucidated the most urgent source of atomization in the field, to which Erixon's article makes oblique but repeated reference. "Much difference of opinion"; "a certain discouragement"; "much has been said": these hints point to the institutional vested interests, interpersonal rivalries, and factionalism that made Western Europe itself a greater challenge than the Cold War to scholarly cooperation. After laying out a massive, ambitious research program, in the last sentence Erixon pricks the balloon with an acknowledgment of human and material constraints: "In the meantime we shall have to limit ourselves to a number of such concrete tasks."

The intellectual program is likewise pragmatic. It draws the widest net possible in order to incorporate existing projects and to make a case for European ethnology as a division of general ethnology, addressing the continent's distinctive social development.[3] Erixon's delineation of activities for the field is more aggregated than integrated, although the core is an effort to merge Swedish-style folklife studies with the compatible holistic and diffusionist tendencies in U.S. anthropology. In consequence, the next ten years of the Journal are heavy on vocabularies of plowing, typologies of haystacks, and other potential contributions to the European atlas Erixon dreamed of. But room is made for new currents: considerations of *Folklorismus* (e.g. Bausinger, Weber-Kellermann), of urban migrants (Esteva-Fabregat), of ethnocentrism and empathy (Niederer), and more. In keeping with Erixon's efforts, the journal was inclusive where inclusion was feasible.

Erixon's reconfiguration was countered by another vision in the very next article of the first issue. In "Altérité et dénivellement culturels dans les sociétés dites supérieures" (1967), the Italian ethnologist Alberto Mario Cirese proposed a different style of remediation: not the integration of European research into general ethnology, but rather an autonomous principle of *découpage*, a demarcation of the field as a distinctive subject with a distinctive theoretical framework. In an explicit conception of disciplinarity, Cirese insists that a true science has not only methods but clear goals and clear boundaries.[4]

Startlingly, Cirese's point of departure for constructing such a science is not ethnology but the far more compromised field of folklore. Naturally he dismisses the existing legitimations of the field as devoted either to romantic imaginings of the "people" or to fetishized historical survivals. Equally – and surely addressing his colleagues in the new journal – he insists that mere "disciplinary patriotism," or the desire to perpetuate one's own institutional base and formation, will not do. Formed as a Socialist militant for whom collecting folksongs was part of a progressive cultural agenda, Cirese followed other Italian scholars of the period in taking his inspiration from Antonio Gramsci's fragmentary "Observations on Folklore." Accordingly, Cirese's *Ethnologia Europaea* article defines our field as the study of "cultural alterity and unevenness in the so-called superior societies."[5]

Like other contributors to the first issue, Cirese is interested in the distinctiveness of Europe, which he defines in institutional and political terms. Europe is organized into centralized states with a nationalist ideology – "the will to recognize themselves as more or less homogeneous historical unities" – and integrated communications. The seeming paradox to be explained is that these same societies exhibit significant internal cultural differentiation. Demonstrating that his paradigm is implicit in existing scholarly conceptions, Cirese reveals a submerged pragmatism suggesting the compatibility of his agenda and Erixon's. At the same time, he sweeps aside old debates by insisting that the objects of ethnology be defined according to the circumstances of their use rather than their production. Regardless of its origin, a given practice may differ "objectively and subjectively" from those recognized and sustained by the official culture, by virtue of its social positioning within a given setting.

Presented by Cirese with no explicit Marxist framing beyond the reference to Gramsci, the new paradigm would seem promising. It resonates with Erixon's attention to social complexity and cultural contact as the hallmarks of a modernized field. Equally, it is compatible with the U.S. turn toward context and performance. As we know, however, it did not achieve hegemony. A parallel development of Gramsci would emerge in British cultural studies with Raymond Williams' formulation of "residual" and "emergent" practices (1977); related conversations took shape around the postcolonial situation in Latin American thought and in India's Subaltern Studies group. In the late 1970s, these lineages came to meet the theorizing from the U.S.-Mexican border inaugurated by Américo Paredes, with José Limón taking the lead in presenting the international work to U.S. folklore scholars (e.g. 1983). Nonetheless, Cirese's program remains an unrealized potentiality, stymied by conscious rejection and even more by inertia. Heterogeneity of topic, approach, and justification has prevailed on both sides of the Atlantic.

Still today, echoes of Erixon and of Cirese are heard every time the state of our field(s) is discussed, most recently in a special issue of *Narodna umjetnost* drawn from the 2015 SIEF congress in Zagreb. The first two articles send us back to the future while setting important agendas for the present. Fabio Mugnaini lays out the "systematization of Gramsci's legacy" in Italian folklore studies to argue the need for ongoing attention to the political character of folklore (Cirese's "differentiation"). This, he insists, must be our response to the institutionalization of "intangible cultural heritage," with its detachment of practices from persons and social situations (2016).

Immediately afterwards, Laurent-Sébastien Fournier reflects on the 2009 creation of the Association Française d'Ethnologie et d'Antropologie, an umbrella organization for smaller associations and initiatives intended to increase their representational power in the French research establishment (2016). He elucidates the dualist tension between unitarism and federalism in the French association, noting parallels in SIEF's conjunction of folklore and ethnology and in the potential accommodation of the two global anthropological unions, the World Council of Anthropological Associations and the International Union of Anthropological and Ethnological Sciences. (We could add the U.S.-European relationship to that list, and Canadian scholars might make further additions.) Drawing on Georg Simmel, Fournier observes that conflicts among intimates are typically more intense than those among strangers; in our case they frequently take the guise of assigning moral weight to methodological differences. A reflexive approach would recognize these conflicts as an index of relationship, while acknowledging their costs as we face the common challenge of maintaining an institutional presence in a climate of scarcity. Like Erixon, Fournier sees cooperation as a precondition of progress, institutional or intellectual.

In Lévi-Strauss's terms, Cirese is an engineer and Erixon is a bricoleur (1962). Cirese constructs coherence out of first principles, organizing the phenomena around them. Intellectually impressive, his article does not tell us how the move to a unified paradigm is to be brought about in practice. Erixon, on the contrary, begins with the institutional and, more discreetly, the interpersonal challenges, coordinating existing resources to arrange a workable solution, though with little by way of a compelling vision.

In the context of university restructuring and a decline in research funding, disciplinary bricolage is inevitable. Its tactics may not be productive. Some of us will hoard our inherited intellectual resources and cling to any available institutional footing, however compromised. Others will run after the next new thing (or the last new thing). We are only human, after all, and our energies are limited. With our efforts dispersed across the "vastness" that Erixon first raised as a problem, fragmentation would seem inescapable. And naturally multiple perspectives have their advantages: this would be made clear by the postmodern critics of the normal science so dear to our colleagues in the 1960s. As a centripetal counterweight to all this centrifugal force, however, we have our learned societies and our journals. *Ethnologia Europaea*, now collaborating with its former antagonist SIEF, is prominent among them. It would seem critical that we supplement the "big tent" approach of inclusivity with actively shepherded conversations across our positions. Calling ourselves back at regular intervals to attend to one another and to rediscover the subterranean linkages between our diverse external manifestations, we can still work to realize what Cirese defined (1967: 12) as our "elementary scientific duty, that of cooperating in general scientific progress."

Notes

1 Published the next year in book form as Bauman & Paredes (1972); see Shuman & Briggs (1993) for an important contextualization and reevaluation of the volume.

2 In Richard Dorson's famous phrase.

3 Folklore and oral tradition are avoided, because of the SIEF split, but gradually make their way back into the journal.

4 Alberto Mario Cirese's article is available on http://www.mtp.dk/details.asp?ELN=500461

5 All translations are mine.

References

Bauman, Richard & Américo Paredes (eds.) 1972. *Toward New Perspectives in Folklore*. Austin: The University of Texas Press.

Bausinger, Hermann 1968–69: Zur Theoriefeindlichkeit in der Volkskunde. *Erixoniana, Ethnologia Europaea* 2–3, 55–58.

Cirese, Alberto Mario 1967: Altérité et dénivellement culturels dans les sociétés dites 'supérieures.' *Ethnologia Europaea* 1, 12–29.

Erixon, Sigurd 1967: European Ethnology in Our Time. *Ethnologia Europaea* 1, 3–11.

Fournier, Laurent-Sébastien 2016: Bringing Together Anthropology, Ethnology, and Folklore: From Factions to Union. *Narodna umjetnost* 53, 43–59.

Kirshenblatt-Gimblett, Barbara 1998: Folklore's Crisis. *Journal of American Folklore* 111, 281–327.

Lévi-Strauss, Claude 1962: *La pensée sauvage*. Paris: Plon.

Limón, José 1983: Western Marxism and Folklore: A Critical Introduction. *Journal of American Folklore* 96, 34–52.

Mugnaini, Fabio 2016: The Haunted Discipline: On the Political Nature of Folklore and the Political Destiny of its Study. *Narodna umjetnost* 53, 15–42.

Rogan, Bjarne 2008: The Troubled Past of European Ethnology: SIEF and International Cooperation from Prague to Derry. *Ethnologia Europaea* 38, 66–78.

Shuman, Amy & Charles L. Briggs 1993: Introduction to special issue, *Theorizing Folklore: Toward New Perspectives on the Politics of Culture. Western Folklore* 52, 109–134.

Williams, Raymond 1977: *Marxism and Literature*. Oxford: Oxford University Press.

Dorothy Noyes is Professor in the Departments of English and Comparative Studies at the Ohio State University. Her most recent book is *Humble Theory: Folklore's Grasp on Social Life* (Indiana University Press, 2016).
(noyes.10@osu.edu)

EUROPEAN ETHNOLOGY IN OUR TIME

Reprinted from *Ethnologia Europaea* 1, 1967

Sigurd Erixon

This opening essay of the then newly founded journal *Ethnologia Europaea* surveys the heterogeneous disciplinary landscape of the field which constitutes its target audience. Situating the field within anthropology, it argues for tolerance of the various kinds of ethnology being pursued in different institutions in Europe, from universities to museums, in order to be able to join forces. All are engaged in folklife research (folklife being equivalent to social life), whose task is to elucidate culture and its role in life as well as the influence of life on the development of culture. The article closes with remarks on method. [Abstract and keywords added by the editors 2017]

Keywords: European ethnology, disciplinary history, anthropology, folklife research

Before we begin to analyse the present conditions and the future possibilities of European ethnology we wish to recall the vast research work which is going on in various countries in this field of study and which we hope will be brought according to plan to a successful end.

There is at present much difference of opinion in our field. Even the term of ethnology has met with opposition in certain quarters, where the need of a universal term has not been understood. However, the field of ethnology is vast and must allow a great variety of conceptions. We are a little worried, though, by a certain discouragement which is found here and there. Some have even felt tempted to reject most of what we have achieved until now and to claim an ethnology that implies either a transition to and acceptance of some or other of our neighbouring sciences or else abstractions or pure indifference. Circumspection and balance are certainly required here.

Every country and every independent territory has its own history and therefore also to a certain degree its own ethnology. The same applies, or should apply to research workers and their schools. The scientific results that have been achieved in different countries demand attention and a fair appraisement. This may be very difficult, especially with regard to smaller countries. Translations or summaries in one of the principal languages are not sufficient. It will be necessary to supervise, bring together and utilize what is produced. For this we need much more than bibliographies. We also need excerpts, organs to treat the material with the general aims clearly set out, as well as modern documentary methods.

Ethnology as a subject of study is represented in very different ways in different countries. Some-

Sigurd Erixon 2017: European Ethnology in Our Time. Reprinted from 1967 *Ethnologia Europaea* 1, 3–11.
Ethnologia Europaea 47:1, 11–17. © Museum Tusculanum Press.

times there is no academic teaching, sometimes it is combined with some other subject, in other cases it has its own chairs, sometimes even special professorships for different branches of the subject. In Sweden European ethnology is represented by independent chairs at the universities of Stockholm, Lund and Uppsala, under the name of "Nordic and comparative folklife research" ("nordisk och jämförande folklivsforskning"). In Finland and Norway we find a differentiation with separate professorships for ethnology, folklore, and social ethnology. The faculty of humanities at Stockholm University has contemplated organizing a special department for anthropologic studies, which should include Nordic and comparative folklife research, general ethnology, and history of religion, including psychology of religion. If this project is realized, other allied subjects may be added. This might be a good solution and mark our European line of thought as opposed to the American, where anthropology is kept together as one subject embracing a great many specialities within its field of study, such as physical anthropology, linguistics, sociology, archaeology, etc.

For the rest, the scientific work in Europe is carried on by museums and archives. Special scientific institutions for studying and publishing the materials are usually lacking, at least in Sweden. In this respect private enterprise has borne the main burden. A great difficulty is the lack of financial means. Neither institutions nor research workers can afford at present to carry out their projects to any larger extent or to undertake new, comprehensive investigations. Instead, they are forced to simplify matters. Often research workers are obliged to accept appointments with institutions and business firms for the sake of special investigations. Others go in for popularizing. Nothing of this is in itself an evil but has a tendency to influence research workers and thus to modify the science.

Nordic or European folklife research in Sweden has its roots in the Renaissance period, with the *Historia de Gentibus Septentrionalibus* (History of the Northern peoples) of Olaus Magnus as a monumental introduction. Thereafter the subject has slowly progressed with several outstanding representatives, but it achieved an independent position only in the first half of this century. Surveys of its older history in Sweden have been published, for example in *Folk-Liv* 1962–65. A summary of important achievements in our field during the twentieth century was given in *Schwedische Volkskunde* (Swedish ethnology), printed in 1961. In *Gwerin, a Journal of Folk Life* for 1962 a survey of my own works since 1912, when the so-called village investigations started, and of the relations of folklife research to general ethnology is printed. Our folklife research has during this century proceeded by stages, each decade has had its own major problems to deal with, which by no means implies indifference to or ignorance of current debates on principles.

At first Nordic folklife research devoted itself exclusively to rural life and its sphere of ideas, since the peasant class was less affected by changes than the others and since its communities and milieus presented the stable order and conformity to tradition which was a condition whilst the new science was being built up. But quite soon we progressed further and besides rural life we have also investigated the life and conditions of the working-class, both in the country and in the towns. Much has been done with regard to the conditions of industry, trade and crafts as well as those of towns and villages. The Laps have aroused interest from early times and have been studied and described, intermittingly from the seventeenth century. These studies have greatly stimulated both Nordic ethnology and European ethnology in general. An important chapter is social life. As modern Swedish sociology, which made its appearance comparatively late, has in general abandoned the historical aspects and concentrated upon present times, folklife research has taken charge of certain sides of the historical development in this field. During the last decades cultural geography has penetrated into the field of folklife research and taken a lively interest in our investigations of such settlements as villages and hamlets. All this makes our own work easier.

A uniform European folklife research in systematic form, taking Europe as a whole, does not yet exist, in spite of many attempts and contributions to this end. Arthur Haberlandt ventured on a general survey in his *Die volkstümliche Kultur Europas in ihrer geschichtlichen Entwicklung*, in connection with Michael Haberlandt's, his father, more superficial survey of the Indo-European peoples in Buschan's *Illustrierte Völkerkunde* of 1926. It was, however, only a kind of introduction and was never carried on or made complete. Better situated in this respect are certain groups of states with cognate languages where several research workers have managed to achieve results also of general importance. Linguistics however have had the great advantage of clear boundaries and a firm basis thanks to the phonetic laws which were launched above all by the brothers Grimm.

The need of a systematic cooperation within ethnology has long been felt in Europe. Already ten years after World War I the CIAP was founded and did some good work. Among other things a number of special committees were constituted. Then World War II came and destroyed the majority of these. Many joint enterprises organized since the war have been supported by Unesco. Much has been said about the activity of the CIAP after the last war. The congresses of the international anthropological union, which recently has shown a new understanding for European ethnology, have usually had a section for Europe. At the International Congress of Anthropological and Ethnological Sciences in Moscow, in 1964, it was decided to extend the collaboration to the whole of Europe and to arrange as soon as possible special conferences for different branches. On that occasion, however, the main principles and needs of European ethnology with regard to organization were overlooked.

In Sweden, European ethnology is usually defined as a branch of general ethnology though without any identification. In this connection, European folklife research, however, holds a special position in having for its subject an extremely sundered part of the world, with only vague remnants of comparatively primitive survival cultures. For the rest it is mainly concerned with mixed circles, stagnating domains and eventually the varying manifestations and fields of activity of the general development, where we deal both with the current of time and changes and with human stability and traditions.

European ethnology deals with given human material, and with a much larger amount of historical awareness and traditional learning than is usually to be found, with exception made, perhaps, for the more learned classes of China and India. It is also concerned with areas, where progress at least in certain parts, has proceeded at a varying but uninterrupted rate and where we usually do not find completely stagnated or special kinds of degenerated forms, such as occur in primitive cultures outside Europe. We have to reckon with a continuous influence from centres of different kinds, also with a central direction from authorities and institutions as well as from leading circles, at the same time as economy and technique become more and more systematized and developed. On this basis, research must perform its work, that is collect its data, systematize the materials, plan distribution and connections. Problems of diffusion and ways of communication are of utmost importance.

General anthropology has gone through a striking development during the last half century. It has dealt with nearly all primitive folk-groups and cultures and furthermore made serious attempts to integrate the results with a view to bringing out, on an abstract level, the conditions of human life universally and as a whole. To become a guiding science is the ambition of general anthropology. The only question is whether this will be possible. The opinions differ as to that. The multitude of new and sometimes even conflicting ideas forces criticism or acceptance, or else in some cases evasion and specialization upon some special matters.

The old colonial powers, such as England, France, Germany, Portugal and Italy, have achieved most important results. Also Denmark and Russia have made important contributions. At times, Austria has taken a leading position. Still, it is the United States that have taken the lead. An outline of what general and European ethnology have in common is given in the international dictionary of Åke Hultkrantz.

Radcliffe Brown urged ethnologists to seek the universal which he regarded as the original. But this is true only in certain cases. There are cases of general likeness that are due to simplification, wear and degeneration. As an example I take the phenomenon called "offerkast", a heap of stones or wooden sticks thrown together on the ground near dangerous passes, for example in the mountains, or at places where accidents and deaths have occurred. It seems evident now that in such cases older and richer offering ceremonies have been simplified or vulgarized into this universal manifestation.

Tylor inspired the idea of culture as being an internally coherent unit, an idea which through Malinowski's influence was then taken up in the United States, where it was further discussed together with an analysis of balancing conditions and models. Malinowski's hostility towards the idea of historical derivations and relations outwards were mainly due to the fact that he was working with isolated island cultures, where such evidences of influences were lacking. On the contrary, these are usually to be reckoned with.

Whether we consider von Luschan's levelling and recurrence or Lévi-Strauss' transformation mechanisms, new likenesses may arise. For the rest development depends on normal cultural relations, meetings with other culture circles, and in later times influence from superior cultures with acculturation as a consequence. Research committees are certainly required to estimate this. Some are already working. In Europe they exist only with regard to some special or some smaller areas. But even a small piece of work in a small area may be a useful building-stone in a greater construction, and guidance and system are necessary.

Fortunately the essential historical material has been collected. The enormous work involved in collecting the material and arranging it in categories and groups according to functions and similarity, in determining it with regard to time, place, and social position, in making comparisons and juxtapositions, also on a social level, and in solving the problems concerning tradition and origin as well as surviving connections, all this can only be touched upon here.

An important chapter concerns the methods used for collecting material: visits, studies, and interviews in the field, questionnaires or direct correspondence. The questionnaire method has been much used in Sweden ever since 1630. Vast collections of scientific material are stored and filed in many European countries. All forms of documentation are being used.

On the whole the research tasks may be divided into groups which deal with either life, society, culture, or the individual. To life belong the ways and conditions of human life (cf. *Folk-Liv* 1962–65). Unfortunately it is not possible to neglect the biological side. Life is a whole. Knowledge of life and its different aspects is indispensable both for comparisons and for abstract epitomes. In northern Europe ethnology has launched the term of folklife, which means that part of life which is due to social transmission and contact. In other words, folklife is social life.

It is the task of folklife research to elucidate culture and its role in life as well as the influence of life on the development of culture. What is culture then? Kroeber's and Kluckhohn's explanation in their great analysis may be formally accepted. Here folklife and culture are juxtaposed, though culture is not fundamentally kept apart from the concept of nature. On this point a complement is necessary in my opinion: nature and culture are two different concepts. Culture was created by man. It is another alternative than the biological in the great process of life, connected just as much with the past and the present as with the future. Culture is specially meant to be a source of help or happiness for the future. It is, for us, something material, mental, and social. It consists as much of memory as of plans for the future and tradition. It is ideas, symbols and technique. It is tool and product and capacity in the work which lies in between. It is the human means of transforming terrain and environment and of creating new forms for human subsistence. It is also custom and feasting. It is fashions and forms. The ready, the formed, the hinted are also culture, on condition that interpretation or explanation go with it. It is training according to patterns given, and so on. The transformation from culture into folk culture occurs in different ways. There exists a mobile culture, as is the case, either for example in the shape of recently created technical culture or propaganda and trade. In this, the special upper classes are generally consumers. Society stores culture reserves in its arsenals. They are sometimes forgotten but may be revived and even used again, if the way of using them is self-evident or directions for their use are given or can be found. Culture must be maintained by work, sometimes by struggle. The historical development must be investigated by means of material in archives, museums and other depots and also interpreted field work. Nowadays experiments are occasionally used in connection with this, at least with regard to certain elements.

There is also a social culture, or culture in and through society. That is something else than "socio-culture" according to Gjessing, who with this concept seems to mean folklife as a whole.

Society is often based on a concrete foundation with a division and grouping determined by natural and historical conditions. On this foundation social life continues, with its groupings, interchanges, systems of compulsions. With reference to them, terms and aspects of varying kind have often been applied, with clear distinctions. This is particularly the case, I think, with Ferdinand Tönnies' concepts of *Gemeinschaft* and *Gesellschaft*. The former, which would correspond to Durkheim's Horde, can hardly be applied to any concrete case in contemporary Europe. We also find, that the English terms of society and community are commonly used regardless of their abstract sense, which is proved by several American and English social anthropologists, who have also made clear, that the term of society in ethnologic literature has a vague, even varied meaning. I refer for example to G.P. Murdock and I. Schapera. The conclusion is that there is no longer any correspondence between the holistic social concept of society on one side, and the phenomenon which Tylor calls culture or complex whole, on the other side, nor Leslie Brown's social system and social structure, nor Malinowski's integral, which in modern anthropology in the United States is called a "holist entity". The American anthropologist Kroeber pointed out that culture must not simply be regarded as the common property of society, it is a system of its own with indistinct social demarcation outwards. The integral was regarded by Malinowski as an automatically formed apparatus, in which human beings are inserted to realize their cultural life by groups. Redfield has said, that the medium does not receive the novelties as a whole and that these are gradually reshaped. This will lead to groups within the group. The word of group is the abstract expression for the formation of circles. For the rest the expression lacks special distinctions but it is still indispensable. Fromm, an American socio-psychologist, has said: There is no "society in general, only specific social structures which operate in different ways". Man does not live in a social bath, but in circles, groups, and combinations. Our investigations of villages, families, and societies become, from this point of view, concrete case studies where we try to find out how the different circles cooperate. In the United States anthropologists will nowadays often use the term of constellation. The territorial concept of community means an area. Most productive is the concept of primary group, which was introduced by C.H. Cooley in 1909 to designate human beings who live in physical proximity, more or less in intimate cooperation face to face. All this necessitates control and consideration.

But the study of society also includes other human groups and teams within or including several concrete communities. Here we first of all meet with the family, which in its preliminary type of parents and child is older than culture itself. Fully developed elementary families with two parents may be found also among some species of animals, they are therefore as a type pre-human. Man has then developed and transformed the families whether we think of extended families or other forms with two or more wives or two or more husbands, etc. Everything connected herewith as well as the introductory stages of marriage and the different stages of life until death exemplify how society is composed both of biological and social matter. More specifically ethnologic are many groupings of a more instable character and permanence which give life its shape and which, in spite of their vagueness, are of a decisive importance for subsistence. Here research has to be done more as a field work, since it is not self-evident.

Every social group has its own pattern of activities, value norms and prestige viewpoints, but, in addition, also a representative upper layer which indicates much of what prestige demands. In the compulsory system of society there are also divisions into layers and groups with regard to economic, mental and cultural character. Many cultural phenomena may be explained with regard to their development through their transmission from one social milieu to another, which corresponds to acculturation.

The destiny of man follows the course of history and the same is true of culture, the equipment and training of man, and also of society. It is the changes of social structure as a consequence of the direction of the inner balance that constitutes the basis of the structure study and of the models belonging to it. "Folk" is synonymous with the adjective "social" and indicates that it refers to the manifestations of human life. "Folklife" thus is social life in its various shades. Foster has defined the European village society as representing a halfculture, as it has been depending on superior units. The term may not be quite satisfactory but it is correct so far as in Europe it is usually a matter of communities and individuals in tribes or states with super- and subordination. This is, however, not the same thing as the serfdom and ceremonial system of the feudal culture which is more characteristic of southern and partly central Europe. In northern Europe the development passed, where the guild system did not exercise its influence, from a more or less primitive village organization directly to forms regulated by military or centrally directed principles.

We do not reckon with a uniform and homogenous upper layer having an individualistic culture. Instead we have what I would like to call active separatist groups with leading functions from a mental or at least organizational point of view. The upper class as such is in this case more a consumer than a producer.

Cities and larger centres demand a specialized ethnology which more belongs to the study of modern time.

Specialization has played a decisive role both in society and for the development of culture. It leads to a state of things that differs from the older conditions of man with their multiplicity of duties and participation in the development of culture. It requires other methods than those used for the investigation of older periods and traditional culture.

What is now required is above all a study of the material culture both on a concrete and on an abstract level and in its relation to custom and spheres of ideas.

In this connection we will also have to take up the study of individuals. The individual is the only independent organism and he is, as Linton has stressed, the really creative factor. Since systematic studies concerning both man and culture deal with the relations between individual, society, and culture, and therefore are standing just in the point of intersection between psychology, sociology, and anthropology, the study of the individual requires cooperation. Before this can be realized, ethnology has to study individuals both from the outside, and through their own destiny and experiences. Through his way of living, his division of time, his moves, his products and his consumption, and finally through his conception of things and cultural traditions, the individual represents certain cases which should be studied and then systematized. Here also the individual's status and role may give some clue, like his power of endurance, well-being, and achievements. We also have to reckon with the need of compensation and remuneration as creative factors.

Another method is to study life cases by means of memoirs, diaries, and account books. The same method might also be applied to families, companies, and smaller communities. On the whole the individual case study is one of the most important tasks in present time.

The investigation of our modern time implying an analysis of the present moment, is impossible since nobody can get a survey of a whole community at one and the same moment. Nevertheless it will therefore be necessary to select one special period, and this may be surveyed as a whole in the same way as older periods and be compared with them.

The choice of the methods and instruments to be employed is a delicate one. As the older stratification, the geographic division and different situations and climates have lost their importance, and frontiers and distances are being eliminated, the way is open to a national culture or an even more general culture type. Thereby the heavy burden of making detail investigations of material conditions, techniques and equipment belonging to it is lifted off the shoulders of the ethnologist and he may concentrate upon the distribution, selection and various combinations of the goods of consumption, and taste and preferences on the part of the consumers, whereas the mass production can be analysed in different places. The groups will then become more and more dependent on the way in which reception takes place and on the initiative and capacity of the individuals. But individuals move and are exposed to influences from different parts. We will then turn mainly to samples, case studies, and certain detail problems. Propaganda through mass media may be analysed in principle and also the way in which man may come into possession of the benefits of society, or the contrary. Population problems are growing more important. In certain cases statistics with sampling may be used but only for special purposes.

Ethnology should be in some senses a summary of the results achieved also by its neighbouring sciences with regard to living realities. But not only this. Of course we may also investigate how traditional forms disappear and how others (more or less) arise. Some control may also be required of mental and socio-psychological influences.

These research problems can hardly be solved otherwise than by way of cooperation, some joint publications and division of work with different groups assuming special tasks, as was done already with the bibliography, the atlas, the dictionary, with research on agricultural implements, etc. One example: investigate villages at different places in the world, using the same system with the same questions and maps, then compare the results at conferences, and build up a social study in the ethnological sense. In the meantime we shall have to limit ourselves to a number of such concrete tasks.

Sigurd Erixon (1888–1968), Professor of ethnology in Stockholm and Research Director of the Nordic Museum. Erixon was the founder of *Ethnologia Europaea – Journal of European Ethnology*, as well as of the journals *Folk-Liv* and *LAOS*. Throughout his *oeuvre*, Erixon was devoted to the European atlas project of which the *Atlas över svensk folkkultur* (1957) was a part. Building up a knowledge base on folk-life research in Sweden, Erixon conducted in-depth studies of peasant material culture and social organisation. Among the central works are *Skultuna Bruks historie* (1935).

For further readings, see Karl-Olov Arntsberg 1989: *Utforskaren: Studier i Sigurd Erixons Etnologi*, Carlssons Bokförlag; Bjarne Rogan 2008: From Rivals to Partners on the Inter-War European Scene: Sigurd Erixon, Georges Henri Rivière and the International Debate on European Ethnology in the 1930s. *Arv: Nordic Yearbook of Folklore* 64, 275–324; Bjarne Rogan 2013: Sigurd Erixon on the Post-War International Scene: International Activities, European Ethnology and CIAP from 1945 to the mid-1950s. *Arv: Nordic Yearbook of Folklore* 69, 89–152.

HOUSEHOLD STUDIES "À LA MODE"?
Liv Emma Thorsen's Anthropology of Peasant Familial Labour

Martine Segalen, Professeur émérite, Université Paris Nanterre, Directeur de Ethnologie française

The article by Liv Emma Thorsen published in 1986 echoes the topics of that decade, which was characterized by the project of building an anthropology of Europe by establishing some common questions and references. After decades of material culture studies in relation to museums, collections and exhibitions, those researchers who – depending on their particular institution – called themselves ethnologists, European ethnologists, or Europeanists turned to more general topics, in order to reconnect with the larger domain of anthropology, dedicated to "other" cultures. Researchers like Liv Emma Thorsen studied their own cultures, treating the peasant as the inside "other", whereas anthropologists dealt with the "other" outside of their own cultures. But in producing research on their own societies, ethnologists endeavored also to set their work in a comparative framework, thus participating in what has been for a long time a far-reaching goal, the construction of an anthropology of Europe.[1] Later on, ethnologists were accused of having "primitivized" Europe and European societies, inasmuch they were working on villages or on marginal cultures, but in the years of their writing they were partaking in a very vivid domain, investigating for instance the family through the lenses of the domestic domain, its role division or the devolution patterns. Thorsen's paper, which is also exceptionally well written, with a rich ethnography and a longitudinal perspective, fits perfectly to the discussions of those years, each study of this kind bringing more material to build upon.

I must confess that there might also be some nostalgia on my part, considering the fact that the rural household as a socio-anthropological domain is no longer *à la mode*. Thorsen echoes directly my own interests concerning the organization of farm production and reproduction as it involves the sex roles division of tasks and responsibilities. (And I may add that re-reading the paper, I was not displeased to discover that my own work was quoted, though I swear I did not know it when I made the choice!) Thorsen's article is also representative in that it reflects the specific moment when anthropology met history through the study of family, and specifically *l'histoire des mentalités*, which was at its pinnacle in that decade. As a matter of fact, one may notice that the references quote Ariès, Le Goff, and Nora, but do not mention the anthropological works of those like Meyer Fortes or Jack Goody, which could have offered another perspective.

The paper also seems indicative of the development of *Ethnologia Europaea* in those years, with more papers in English than in German, thus opening itself to a larger audience. It testifies to the focus of the journal in the 1980s and 1990s before it moved to other topics, when it became more attuned also to the questions of general anthropology or cultural studies. However, if this article (along with a few others) is a good testimony of what often interested ethnologists and anthropologists then, namely,

Martine Segalen 2017: Household Studies "à la mode"? Liv Emma Thorsen's Anthropology of Peasant Familial Labour.
Ethnologia Europaea 47:1, 18–20. © Museum Tusculanum Press.

the effects of technical changes within the domestic group, it also opens new perspectives. The village is at the center, but the analysis is not stuck to the concept of "traditional society". Quite to the contrary, it analyses the consequences of an important episode in the system of food production in Europe, and as such, offers an interesting opening to the study of processual changes implied by "modernity".

The article is innovative in many ways, for example (1) interviewing three generations of women, (2) developing the notion of material culture by applying it to modern machinery, and (3) introducing the concept of "gender", which was only then beginning to be discussed in anthropology, when examining the various relationships between men and women in connection with the various modes of production.

With a fine grained ethnography, the author describes the conditions of work on a Norwegian farm in a small community. Thorsen focuses her attention on the division of work roles. By following three generations of women, the author can show the evolution of mentalities and the conflict of values among the youngest generations when, at the same time, technical modernization and the penetration of new ideas about what should be a woman's role, collided. Thus the author combines successfully different threads of topics that then moved to the core of discussions in the Europeanist social anthropology in the 1990s. The author renovates the theme of material culture, which was the staple of ethnology until the 1970s, in order to settle itself as a scientific discipline, departing from folklore and its romantic flavor. But in doing so, the researchers had forgotten the cultural and social relations transiting through the technical gestures and implements. The paper also reveals the expansion of the new developments introduced by *l'Ecole des Annales* and its *histoire des mentalités*. Changes regarding what is "natural" for a woman in each generation is framed in the concept of *mentalités*, which helps understand the conflicts regarding the sexual division of work when new modern implements enter the farm.

After a theoretical presentation of the concepts of ideology and mentality, the article starts with a general description of the diversity of traditional farming techniques throughout Norway, and of the rigid role division. However, the author explains that there were some variations in this pattern when men were away from the farm to go fishing or if they were employed in forestry. Generally, before commercial farming developed, the female work domain was inside, the male work domain outside. Then the paper describes the consequences of the introduction of the first technical changes, from family production of dairy products to industrial dairies followed by the introduction of mechanical cutting machines at the beginning of the twentieth century, and after World War II of the tractor. The author very interestingly points out that the workload for men was alleviated, whereas the female domestic chores (cooking, washing) was still done without the help of technical implements, these machines arriving only two decades later.

The core of the ethnography delineates the consequences of the acquisition of the milking machine, a technique that impinges on the traditional feminine domain; with its mechanization, the task moves from the feminine to the masculine domain. This acquisition was generally motivated by the fact that men would find it tedious to milk the cows by hand in case their wives were unable to do it. The cowshed, a traditionally feminine space, became masculine as soon as machinery entered it. Thorsen goes on analyzing in a very innovative way the interweaving of time, work, and childcare in farming families and the new conflicts of values the young mothers were confronted with, as new patterns regarding the importance of mothering emerged.

Thus briefly summarized, this paper can be seen as illuminating numerous topics that will be developed further on in other contexts, a new approach to material culture, the opening of the field of gender studies, the discovery of the growing importance of the child.

As a long-time member of the editorial board of *Ethnologie française*, and its director for the past ten years, it is interesting to reflect on the trajectory of both journals. They have followed the changes in the discipline, and the new contexts of its production, and over the years, their contents have evolved enormously. But the mid-1980s, from which Thorsen's article derives, appears in retrospect to be the end of an era. The decade 1990–2000 marks a shift away from studying questions associated with rural societies to analyzing the various facets of modernity, new family patterns in urban areas, sports, politics, contemporary rituals, and in the 2000s the local effects of globalization and *metissages*, while producing a continuous quest about the nature and meaning of the territory called Europe and its identities, the reconfiguration of patrimony, offering a fresh look at ethnographical museum presentations, etc. Symbolically, the change in this journal's contents is manifested by the new cover. After some years with a cover illustrated by the abduction of Europa, since 2005 each issue benefits from a special cover page, some of them being particularly striking (if not shocking: I am thinking of the issue of 2006, 36:2 showing tourists the day after the tsunami sun-bathing among the remnants of the wreck).

The shift toward cognitivism (already present in Thorsen's paper as she talks of the "cognitive structures of the peasant mind") and cultural studies, à la Löfgren and Frykman, has been very present in the pages of the journal for the past 15 years. As a matter of fact, Liv Emma Thorsen's work is an interesting example of a shift in topics while continuing to pursue the same strands. In a paper published in *Ethnologia Europaea* (2012, 42:1, 5–20), "A Supreme Elephant: Movement, Materiality and Mentalities", she examines the "insides" of the process that brings an elephant from former Portuguese West Africa into a Swedish Museum of Natural History. The topic is new, but we see that materiality and mentalities which were dealt with in the 1986 paper are also discussed, an old topic in new garments!

I am in a position to admire the various editors' work, because I know the amount of energy and time which are required to publish a journal, not only to define the grand orientations but to tackle the daily tasks and thousands of details that make a scientific journal worth of that qualification, both within the country and as assessed by international committees (without mentioning the consequences of digitalization, the fast disappearance of the paper issues, the fall in the number of subscriptions which require a new economic model).

Congratulations and happy birthday, *Ethnologia Europaea*, and long live!

Note

1 Cf. Martine Segalen: Quelles Europes pour quelles ethnologies? Le cas de la revue *Ethnologie française*. In: Francis Demier & Elena Musiani (eds.), *L'Europe: Une autre nation?* Nanterre: Presses de l'Université Paris Nanterre, in press.

Martine Segalen, a member of CNRS until 1986, then as a professor at the Université Paris Nanterre, has conducted research on family, kinship, and rituals, both in rural settings and conditions of the changing modernity. Presently, professeur émérite at the same university, she is director and editor-in-chief of *Ethnologie française*.
(msegalen@u-paris10.fr)

WORK AND GENDER

The Sexual Division of Labour and Farmers' Attitudes to Labour in Central Norway, 1920–1980

Reprinted from *Ethnologia Europaea* 16:2, 1986

Liv Emma Thorsen

During the last hundred years, the original low technology agriculture of rural Norway has developed into highly specialized commercial farming. This transformation has been vividly discussed both by historians and ethnologists. A main theme in the debate has been as to which degree new technology and integration of agriculture in market economy have brought about a dissolution of the traditional peasant culture. In the present study of women's work on farms in Central Norway, it is argued that although the material structures of the farms have been subject to important transformations, essential structures such as the sexual division of labour and the ideas constituting the peasant ideal of femininity, hardly changed before the 1960s.

Keywords: women's work, gender, agricultural work, peasant culture, Central Norway

Introduction

The sexual division of labour and peasant society's attitudes to labour discussed in this article[1] are part of a more extensive study of the socialization and the adult life of women on farms in a small community (5,000 inhabitants) in central Norway. The two themes, socialization and adult life, are followed through three generations of women during the period 1920–1980. The analysis is an attempt to evaluate the register of the socialization of girls and of female adult life in relation to the economic and social organization of the farm on one hand, and on the other hand, in relation to traditional attitudes and values in a peasant culture as opposed to the ideologies reigning in the surrounding society.

The aspects of change and continuity in the sexual division of labour are discussed. Special attention is paid to women's work, both farm work and housekeeping including care of the various members of the household, and the relation between technological innovation and division of labour. The second part of the paper deals with the attitudes to labour typically found in the peasant society. These specific attitudes are here labelled "the mentality of work". During the period of study, this mentality of work was challenged by new ideologies of femininity. Of special interest is the part of the femininity ideology concerning motherhood.

Liv Emma Thorsen 2017: Work and Gender: The Sexual Division of Labour and Farmers' Attitudes to Labour in Central Norway, 1920–1980.
Reprinted from 1986 *Ethnologia Europaea* 16:2, 137–148.
Ethnologia Europaea 47:1, 21–29. © Museum Tusculanum Press.

Theoretical Frame-Work

In ethnology, folk culture is studied in the light of three central dimensions: time, space and social stratum. In other words, the ethnologist performs a cultural analysis from a historical perspective. When this discipline was still young, much emphasis was laid on the study of the traditional folk culture, that is the peasant culture. Today the whole spectrum of popular manifestations is part of the ethnologist's field of interest, although contemporary Norwegian ethnology mainly deals with work process studies.

In recent years, however, Norwegian ethnology has taken a new direction of study. The study of material cultural elements has been partially abolished and more emphasis has been put upon the study of so-called cognitive structures of culture.[2] These are the values and attitudes that form the basis of human behaviour. The present analysis of the cognitive structures is based on the bipartition of these structures introduced by the French Annales-school. Thus, an attempt is made to distinguish between the immaterial cultural manifestations whose origin may be attributed to an ideology and those with an origin in a specific mentality. Ideology is conceived as thought and idea systems elaborated by a certain period's intelligentsia and has been rooted in the literary tradition. Mentality is connected to a culture's system of standards and values. Mentality is transferred unconsidered and "unconsciously" and is often connected to a praxis which is considered correct and "natural" by the members of the community. According to the French Annales-tradition, mentality is the part of culture that changes the slowest (Blom 1986; Le Goff & Nora 1985). Ideology may prove to have such an impact that in time it will become a part of the mentality (Rosenbeck 1985). An illustrative example is the Victorian conception of femininity in which culturally founded female characteristics were considered to be of natural origin. Since then, Western women have been oppressed by a myth proclaiming that the women's body and mind primarily are intended for the reproductive or generative purpose (Hausen 1981: 56).

Applying the theoretical categories of ideology and mentality on the empirical material, the ethnologist may be able to show whether the immaterial innovations in the adult lives of women on farms give rise to opposition, or if they are accepted and assimilated by these women.

The Traditional Norwegian Peasant Culture: Some Characteristics

Traditional Norwegian peasant culture prior to today's specialized, commercial farming (that is before 1860) is little known outside Scandinavia, so in the following paragraphs a brief description intended to serve as back-ground information for the further presentation of my case-study will be given.

Traditionally, the division of labour between men and women in peasant society was very clear-cut and stable, although we find important, local variations concerning the contents of the female work tasks as opposed to the male ones. These variations may find their explanations in peasant economy, which was – and still is – based on the exploitation of different resources dependent on the geographical location of a community. Thus, farming is combined with fishing in the coastal districts and with forestry in the inlands. In this century, a new combination, that of farming and wage labour, has arisen.

Different combinations of economic adaptions have influenced the sexual division of labour as well as the organization of the peasant household and the distribution of authority between husband and wife. Ethnologists distinguish between areas with female peasants and areas with male peasants (Berggreen 1984). Female peasants have predominated in areas where the men left the farms for long periods, for example for fishing or woodcutting. Women with periodically absent husbands had more influence on the management of the farm than their fellow sisters in areas where the men worked on the farm most of the year. The majority of female peasants were found in regions where farms are relatively small, or where arable land is scarce, while male peasants often were found in regions where farms are big and arable land is abundant.

Norwegian agriculture is also characterized by the systematic utilization of vast mountain pastures, that is mountain dairy pasturing (Norwegian:

seterbruk). With some very few exceptions, mountain dairy farming is extinct today. Another characteristic feature of Norwegian agriculture is the isolated farms or small hamlets of single farms (*grend*), as opposed to European village organization.

The alpine cottage (*setra*) was a female domain. An adult woman, sometimes the housewife, was in charge of the dairy work, while a child was herding the animals. This could be a girl or a boy of eight to fifteen years. The dairy products constituted an essential part of the winter food supply and were extremely important for the household. In addition, cheese and butter are some of the few articles that were produced for sale.

The traditional division of labour between men and women on the farm mainly corresponds to the division between outdoor work (*utearbeid*) and indoor work (*innearbeid*), respectively. In other words, men worked outdoors and women worked indoors. The cowshed, the pigsty and the hencoop belonged to the female sphere of work. The horse was the only animal taken care of by the husband himself or by a male servant. It is important to emphasize that women also carried out fieldwork.

This rigid sexual division of labour was manifest in fieldwork too. As a rule, women never ploughed or sowed in regions where male farming predominated. However, they did heavy work like picking stones from the fields and cutting cereals. Men never participated in the indoor work.

Sexual Division of Labour ca. 1920–1960[3]

Even up to the period between the two wars, the children growing up in peasant households were socialized into a division of labour that closely resembled the traditional one known from regions with male peasants. The farmer himself was the head of fieldwork, while the wife and the children were assistants doing the nontechnical work. The cutting of cereals was female work as long as it was carried out by hand, but when cutting machines were introduced, it passed to the male domain. Already in the beginning of the twentieth century, mountain dairy farming had been abandoned. Thus in the period under observation, dairy production and production of refined milk products had been taken over by proper dairies. Therefore, women no longer had the dairy farm as their domain. The new system implied that the milk was delivered to the dairy, but it also required that the women had to pay more attention to the quality of the milk. As the production of milk grew more important in the total economy of the farm, the work in the cowshed increased, in spite of the fact that the refining of the milk was done in the dairies.[4] The change from mountain dairy farming to dairy industry is an important trait of the first technological transformation of agriculture.

During the first half of this century, the number of farm workers[5] employed in agriculture decreased, and in the 1950s, many married couples were alone with their daily work on the farm. Seasonal labour, however, was still hired to do fieldwork. Today, the number of farm workers in Norwegian agriculture is almost non-existent. The second technological transformation of agriculture started in the 1940s with the introduction of new agricultural machinery, the tractor being the most important new piece of farming equipment. The technological household revolution did not take place until the 1960s.[6] Therefore, in the period 1940–1960, approximately, we observe an unbalance in the burden of labour between the two sexes, in the disfavour of the women.

Rigidity or Flexibility in the Sexual Division of Labour? Superiority and Inferiority

The farm traditionally was a unity with a rigid division of labour between the sexes. Both men and women were expected to master certain skills by virtue of their gender. There are, however, numerous examples of a crossing of the borderline between male and female work, especially in relation to fieldwork. The borderline between the two sexes' fields of activity becomes somewhat less distinct when we follow the children in their tasks. Small boys were doing textile work like carding, and they also assisted their mother in the cowshed doing the cleaning and feeding, but rarely the milking. In households with only girls, the daughters accompanied their father in the traditional male fieldwork. But children growing up in households with both girls and boys were socialized into the adult division of labour from an early age. The girls followed their mother in their work, and the boys had the father as their teacher. So the girls, among other tasks, did housework as a favour to their brothers.

As we have seen, the division of work was rigid. On the other hand, it was also characterized by the flexibility displayed by one sex. The women had to subordinate themselves to the leadership of the farmer whenever the labour in the fields required more hands. This flexibility manifested itself through the women's praxis of postponing parts of the housekeeping during the labour intensive summer season. In my opinion, this feature justifies that an interpretation of the relationship between the sexes be held in terms of patriarchy. This patriarchy interpretation is sustained by the fact that the majority of women who married a farmer in the years between the wars and in the 1950s were denied any information of or influence upon the management of the farm. The higher prestige of the male work can also be seen from the way the crossing of the borderlines in the sexual division of labour was sanctioned: A woman who mastered a man's work was held in esteem but at the same time the label "mannishness" was attached to her person while a man was considered ridiculous if he performed a woman's work.

The following quotation from an interview with a woman born in 1919, will illustrate the female subordination:

> Interviewer: Do you think we have got more equality between husband and wife?
> Interviewed: Yes, no doubt, and, you know, before my time, they were afraid of their husbands. They had to do things exactly as they knew they [the husbands] wanted it to be done.
> [...] I know somebody, it might be from my parents' generation, where the wives left the cowshed to pour coffee for their husband. They left the cow they were milking! Because they had to see to it that the cup was not empty! It was not common, but I know it happened.

As late as the 1960s, one can distinguish between two separate work hierarchies as a function of gender, the women's being subordinate to the men's. While growing up, girls had to obey the adult women in the household, mainly their mother. The superior authority, however, was held by the father. A majority of young wives worked together with their mother-in-law for some years, the latter being the head of the female hierarchy as long as the young wife's father-in-law remained in charge of the management of the farm. When the authority was transferred to his son, the young wife attained the peak of her female career as a farm woman. It was she who now was in charge of the female work on the farm, but she had no authority when it came to the management of the land, the forest or the means of production. Of course individual differences occurred: Some women were strong enough to claim their rights. Those who have succeeded in breaking the male dominance, are often female allodialists.[7]

The Milking Machine: An Example of both Change and Continuity in the Sexual Division of Labour

The story of the introduction of the milking machine is an example of how technological innovation may cause a break in the tradition, but it also illustrates how an innovation may contribute to sustaining the traditional division of labour. Finally, the introduction of the milking machine is also an example of a correspondence between the introduction of a piece of new technology and of men taking over female work. The milking machine, and together with the machine, the man, entered the cowshed in the 1940s and 1950s.

Until then, the cowshed and all the work connected with the care of the animals' feeding, watering, cleaning and milking was female work. To become an efficient hand milker, one must be trained from an early age. An untrained person is not able to do this kind of work. As time goes by, this heavy work puts a strong stress on arms and hands, and aged women are often troubled with pains in their arms because of the hand-milking they have been doing for years and from the age of approximately eleven.

The refining of milk was taken over by dairies

already in the beginning of this century. This is an indication of the increased economic importance of animal husbandry. In spite of this it is a fact that the women went on to do the tedious milking.[8] Why was it so? Did the men acquire an interest in the cowshed and the production of milk for the mere reason that with modern technology the work could be done quicker and easier?

The story concerning why their husband bought a milking machine is remembered by all the informants who have experienced the transition from hand milking to mechanical milking. Very often this is the story about the wife who falls ill and remains incapable of doing the work in the cowshed for some time. Her husband tries for a short while to do the job, but being untrained with the milking, he fares poorly. The story ends with the purchase of the machine.

The women who are telling the story do not attribute any importance to the fact that in this way their husbands took over some of the work that earlier belonged to them. Rather they stress the point that generally, men never accepted doing female work in the cowshed as long as this work was manual. The second point which throws light on the agrarian patriarchy, is this: Many women express clearly that this is one of few examples of their husbands being willing to spend money on something that would reduce the women's burden of labour. The reason the women give for this, is, that in actual fact their husbands bought the machines because of their own needs.

But why did the men not simply hand over the milking machine to the women the way they later handed over the washing machine, for instance? Why did the men increase their actual field of work, and why did the women consent to having their field of work restricted? I have no full explanation of this so far, but some reasons will be suggested in the following paragraphs:

1. The female labour was still heavy and exhausting as most of the work was done by hand. Both men and women agree that the women had the longest working day at this time.
2. In the beginning of the twentieth century, milking and the rest of the work in the cowshed had been the job of the maid. On smaller farms, however, this work was done by the housewife or one of her daughters. As the number of servants decreased, this work in the cowshed had to be done by the housewife or her daughters. At this time, the indoor work was attributed a higher prestige than the milking. The former and the present paragraph lead to the conclusion that nothing in the women's total situation gave any reason for the women to regret this loss of female domain.
3. The milking machine came into common use at a time when the amount of male work on the farm was reduced as a result of the increased use of machines in the fields. The men suddenly had more time on their hands.

How and where should they invest their spare time? At the farm, there were two places to go: either to the cowshed, or to the dwelling house. Here we must take the traditional border line between male and female work into consideration: The man could not pass the threshold to do indoor work without losing face. The traditional rigid sexual division of labour with a transition being possible only to the female labour force, has until today served as a mental block against male participation in housekeeping. The cowshed, however, was a zone of transition, even if it traditionally belonged to the female field of activity. It has been pointed out earlier that small boys could do assistant work in the cowshed. And, what is more important, in the last three decades, milk production became of increasing economic importance to the farm and consequently of increasing interest to the farmer himself. In conclusion, the farmer had only one place to go, namely to the cowshed.

Today husband and wife share the care for the animals and the milking at the farms that still have animal husbandry.[9] These women are less peripheral in the farm production than their fellow sisters on farms producing only grain or grass.

Attitudes to Labour

The attitudes to labour will here be regarded as a cultural mechanism that, together with the basic need for food and clothes, kept the peasant family at their work. Finally an attempt will be undertaken to show how farm women in the actual period were torn between work and care.

During the last twenty years, farming in Norway has developed into a profession among other professions. However, farming is still a life-mode that regulates and influences not only the work, but also the private life of the farm household (Højrup 1983). Agriculture differs from other life-moduses in the modern society in that the household is still a unity of work and not only of consumption. Farmers are the only social group in modern Norway that leads a daily life where work and leisure time are still firmly entwined. The farm work must be done, and even if the farmer couple tries to restrict the daily number of working hours, the changing character of the work with highly intensive labour periods during summer in contrast to the more quiet wintertime, makes it difficult to calculate the work in a regular number of hours per day.

In spite of the increasing demands for efficiency and profit today, the women who have been interviewed as a general rule state that they consider themselves satisfied with the peasant way of life. They regard themselves and their husbands as people who are free to work as they like. Nobody tells them what to do, nor when to do it. As they put it, they are "their own masters". On the other hand, there is little choice, since "the farm is our living".

> And the work, ... there is one very important thing, and that is to run the farm properly, to keep it well, and to work hard! That is the nicest thing you can say about a person in the countryside. I think this is specific to the country life. That one is industrious and runs the farm well, and that one is enterprising, so to say. I think they bother less about other personal qualities. That is my point of view. (Woman born in 1956)

This quotation from an interview with a young wife on a farm illustrates a central feature of the mentality in peasant society, that is, the strong importance attributed to work, work being the paramount constituent of life, and the most outstanding human virtues being those of industry and enterprise.

To be a farmer, male or female, is to accept labour as a fundamental condition of life. To many farmers, life is equivalent to work, and vice versa. This profound acceptance of life being equivalent to hard work should be seen in connection with the family's economic strategy. The objective of the project for the future of a young peasant couple "is aimed at creating alliances which ensure accession to ownership of the land, or its development, or yet again to prevent its being broken up" (Segalen 1983: 13). In this strategy, the preservation and the improvement of the farm are paramount, marriage and childbirths being instruments to fulfil the project for the future. The attitudes to labour in the peasant life-mode may be considered components of a "key scenario". The key scenarios of a culture "both formulate appropriate goals and suggest effective action for achieving them, [...] in other words (they are) key cultural strategies" (Ortner 1973: 1341). The attitudes to labour in the present paper labelled "the mentality of work" form part of the cognitive structures of peasant culture.

Contemporary and historical feminist research in Scandinavia parts from a definition of women's work that includes both wage labour, housework and care (Gullestad 1984; Holter 1984). To modern women, the main division in the organization of their daily life is between wage labour and family work, and not between work and leisure time. The conflict between wage labour and family work that many women experience today is well known. Until the last war, female wage labour was more or less restricted to working class women; as wage labour has become common also among middle class women, this conflict is now being paid more attention. The situation of farm women is often forgotten in the debate because their double work is less obvious, and because it is rooted in a different economic organization.

Married women on farms have carried out "institutionalized double work" (Gaunt 1983) insofar as farm work, housework and care have been woven together for centuries. They acquire their profession by marriage, in contrast to other people who normally choose their profession.[10] This must be one of the reasons why so many of the informants define themselves as housewives, although they admit that the work they carry out during a day in many aspects differs from that of a housewife in town. They clearly do not fit into the official categories of profession.

The Farm Women Trapped between Work and Care

> We had a sleeping room and nothing else in the dwelling house. That was all, this was perhaps the worst period. [...] When I think about it now... that even if it did not last for more than five years, I consider it a long time. [...] And you never knew if you did enough. I remember I was out in the field cutting grain. I remember that my mother-in-law carried the baby to me in the field so that he could be nursed. [...] I married in 1948, in April, and after that things happened in rapid succession. The following year in July, that is fourteen months later, I got number two. And it was a difficult time. One sort of had no change to care for oneself or the children. For if one had a couple of hours free, one nevertheless felt that one had to work. In the busy period (summer), I worked in the fields, and my mother-in-law did the cooking. [...] And the children stayed with her. Do you know what was dreadful for me? That was when I came home, and they ran towards me, so that I had to carry them. But being so tired, I nearly fell myself. And they came to us and were happy, you know, because we came home. This was very difficult for me. (Woman born in 1923)

> Interviewer: What did you do when you had small children, did she [the mother-in-law] look after the children while you were out working in the fields, or were you free from doing part of the field work while you had small children?
> Interviewed: No, she preferred not to work outdoors. And I wanted to stay outdoors because I've always liked to work in the open. And the youngest ones stayed with her, but when they grew a bit older, then I brought them with me out into the fields, you know. So after all one has a bit of bad conscience. [...] Today they say their conscience is bad because they take wage labour having small children, but the bad conscience, a farmer's wife had that too, because one was always extremely busy. One had little time for the care of the children. Very little time. Well, and I have told them now after they are grown up, that after all I have a bad conscience, because I never had the time to accompany them anywhere. Or work had to be done in the cowshed, or it was ... there was always something. (Woman born in 1921)

The two quotations illustrate the abovementioned conflict, a conflict that is experienced by many of the interviewed women. They were trapped between the peasant society's expectations of them to be industrious workers, and their own wish for being caregiving mothers. An obvious interpretation of what the women state themselves, is that the general demand on the peasant women to fulfil the ideal of work traditionally has been stronger than the expectations laid upon the woman to care for the emotional needs of the family. At least, the first has been given priority to the second.

The conflict may also be viewed as the emergence of new ideas about mothering and housework among farm women in this period, ideas originally rooted in the dominant culture's ideas and values.[11] In the years between the world wars it became common that girls in the countryside followed courses in housekeeping and infant nursing. In elementary school, at these courses in housekeeping and also in the popular literature, the young girls became acquainted with the bourgeois ideal of femininity. This ideal, however, emanated from a sexual division of labour which was totally unknown to the majority within peasant society until the 1960s and the late modernisation of agriculture. Although the bourgeois female type was held up as an ideal also for peasant women, my assertion is that this female ideal prescribing the woman exclusively to care for the management of the house and the family life, never had a breakthrough. The daily need for labour on the farm, and the "mentality of work", were an efficient hindrance to an ideal of femininity prescribing refinement and fragility. As in French peasant culture as described by Martine Segalen (Segalen 1983: 17), the ideal of femininity among Norwegian peasants was one of laborious women of physical vigour and health.

This was a period of shifting ideas, and many mothers seem to have been torn between the loyalty to the farm that was the living of the family, and the ideal of a modern and sentimental mother, putting more effort into the emotional care of the children than what had been usual in the traditional peasant society. Given the material structures and the division of labour within the family, the women had no objective possibilities to introduce a sentimental praxis.[12]

The new technology, like the milking machine and the household technology of the 1960s, saved time that could be used to care for the family. After 1960, however, we are confronted with a third ideal of femininity which must be understood in the light of postwar education society rather than in terms of the eighteenth century bourgeois female ideal.

Notes

1 Presented as a paper at the XIIIth Rural Sociology Conference, Braga 1–4 April, 1986.
For an extensive discussion of the sexual division of labour and the importance of work related to age and generations in this farming community, see Thorsen 1993: 51–183 and 193–219.

2 Today, thirty years after this article was written, studies of material culture, or materiality, have been proliferating in ethnology and related disciplines as well as in the social sciences.

3 The following discussion of the sexual division of labour and farmers' attitudes to labour is based on oral sources, that is, qualitative interviews with 45 farm women born between 1900 and 1956. The transcriptions of the interviews are 1,700 pages.

4 Avdem (1984) in her study of peasant women's labour in the mountain settlement of Lesja in central Norway, explains thoroughly how women's work concerning the care for the cows and the responsibility of the production of milk, led to an increase in their labour.

5 A farm worker as opposed to a seasonal labourer was employed for a year at a time.

6 The washing machine was the most important technological innovation in the female indoor work. The washing machine had become a common good as late as the 1960s. The freezer put an end to the laborious conservation of food. Many households bought both a washing machine and a freezer within a couple of years of each other.

7 In Norway, the eldest son has had the first right to take over the farm (allodial right). In 1975, a new law assigned the allodial right to the firstborn child irrespective of gender. In a paper presented at this conference, Eldbjørg Fossgard studies the strong opposition to the new allodial law in peasant society.

8 In other West-European countries, like England and Denmark, male specialists took over the work in the cowshed, including milking, in the same period as the dairy products increased in value. In England, milking was male work as early as in the middle of the nineteenth century, in Denmark a couple of decades later.

9 The number of farms in the community with a production based on animal husbandry decreases every year. Those who continue are usually situated in areas not fit for the production of grain in combination with the breeding of pigs.

10 Of course, this choice of profession is limited by factors like family tradition, economy, social class etc.

11 For an introduction to the complex discussion of the ideological change of the conception of the private life, including mothering and family life, refer to Ariès (1963), Frykman (1981), Frykman & Löfgren (1979), Shorter (1976), among others.

12 Sentimental is here given the same meaning as in Shorter (1976).

References

Ariès, Philippe 1960: *L'enfant et la vie familiale sous l'Ancien Régime.* Paris.

Avdem, Anna Jorunn 1984: *... gjort ka gjerast skulle: Om arbeid og levekår for kvinner på Lesja 1910–1930.* Oslo.

Berggreen, Brit 1984: The Female Peasant and the Male Peasant: Division of Labour in Traditional Norway. *Ethnologia Scandinavica*, 66–78.

Blom, Ida 1986: Mentalitetshistorie og kvinnehistorie. *Kvinder – Mentalitet – Arbejde.* Århus. Submitted.

Frykman, Jonas 1981: Pure and Rational: The Hygenic Vision: A Study of Cultural Transformation in the 1930s. The New Man. *Ethnologia Scandinavica*, 36–63.

Frykman, Jonas & Orvar Löfgren 1979: *Den kultiverade människan.* Lund.

Gaunt, David 1983: *Familjeliv i Norden.* Malmö.

Gullestad, Marianne 1984: *Kitchen Table Society.* Oslo.

Hausen, Karin 1981: Family and Role-Division: The Polarisation of Sexual Stereotypes in the Nineteenth Century – an Aspect of the Dissociation of Work and Family Life. In: Evans & Lee (ed.), *The German Family.* London.

Højrup, Thomas 1983: The Concept of Life-Mode: A Form-

Specifying Mode of Analysis Applied to Contemporary Western Europe. *Ethnologia Scandinavica*, 15–51.

Holter, Harriet (ed.) 1984: *Patriarchy in a Welfare Society.* Oslo.

Le Goff, Jacques & Pierre Nora 1985: *Constructing the Past.* London.

Ortner, Sherry B. 1973: On Key Symbols. *American Anthropologist* 75:5, 1338–1346.

Rosenbeck, Bente 1986: Køn og klasse set i relation til mentalitetsforandringer. In: *Kvinder – Mentalitet – Arbejde.* Århus.

Segalen, Martine 1983: *Love and Power in the Peasant Family.* Chicago.

Thorsen, Liv Emma 1993: *Det fleksible kjønn: Mentalitetsendringer i tre generasjoner bondekvinner 1920–1985.* Oslo.

Author's Note to the Reprinted Article

In this reprinted version of the article, I refer to the book based on my dr. philos thesis, *Det fleksible kjønn*, instead of, as in the original version, articles. In the book persons, farms and community are anonymous; I have therefore also omitted names in the reprinted article.

In Norwegian, *bonde* and *bondekvinne* mean both "peasant" and "peasant woman". The use of these terms was not consistent in the original version. I have replaced "peasant woman" with "farm woman", but kept the translation of *bondesamfunn* and *bondekultur* as "peasant society" and "peasant culture".

Liv Emma Thorsen, Professor emerita, Department of Culture History and Oriental Languages, University of Oslo. Her research interests today are the cultural history of animals, and she has been faithful to the study of things throughout her career. In 2014, she published *Elephants Are Not Picked from Trees: Animal Biographies in Gothenburg Natural History Museum* (Aarhus University Press).
(l.e.thorsen@ikos.uio.no)

ETHNOLOGIA NATIONUM
Or, The World as We See It: "strange, but interesting"[1]

Peter Jan Margry, Meertens Institute, University of Amsterdam

What actually constitutes an academic discipline? Being incorporated by academic institutions, described by journals and handbooks, delineated through historiography and reputation? Most importantly, I think, a scholarly field is represented via its practitioners – the active community of scholars themselves. They shape the field, renew it and eventually pass the scientific baton on to younger generations by enthusing and inspiring students. They should create the "charisma" of a discipline that draws students into the field of study.

It was in the late 1990s, as a historian, that I first heard about "European ethnology". I had started working at the Meertens Institute in Amsterdam in the department of *Volkskunde* (Folkloristics). In 1998 – rather late in the European context – this department was renamed *Nederlandse Etnologie* (Dutch Ethnology). I was still puzzled. What did that imply? Was it a specifically Dutch version of ethnology? If so, how did it relate to the international discipline of European ethnology? I was determined to understand this better. My colleagues made the practical suggestion that, for an initial immersion into that renamed field, I check the few handbooks available and browse through the many volumes of a journal that was being published in Copenhagen. I was told that the journal started due to an old scholarly feud between folklorists and ethnologists within the then *Commission internationale des Arts et Traditions Populaires* at Unesco. Comprised mostly of Scandinavians (the name of Sigurd Erixon, the leading ethnologist of the time, was mentioned in that context), the publication continued after the schism as a journal for the ethnology following; most of the folklorists regrouped as the international society SIEF in Athens in 1964.[2] That they had split up, I was told again, was not all that surprising, as Nordic ethnology was known for its modern views and approaches after having reinvented itself by breaking the chains of traditionalist "folkloristic stances".

However, the volumes on the shelf displayed an archaic Latin name as an equivalent for the field of European ethnology: *Ethnologia Europaea*.[3] And again, I thought, what does that mean? I took the first volume from 1967 off the shelf and looked at the first page. To my surprise, the very first lines mentioned a short historiographical contribution by the Dutch professor August Bernet Kempers, dealing with the *Volkskunde* in the Netherlands.[4] As it was published in this very first volume, it felt reassuring that research done in the Netherlands was indeed a part of European ethnology. This was confirmed by the fact that Bernet Kempers later became a professor of European ethnology himself.[5] The browned pages of the first journal volumes also made clear that those issues dated back many years. The various historiographical and discipline-focused contributions, relevant in a time frame of establishing, defining, and distinguishing European ethnology as a reinvented discipline, had lost the topicality of their time.

I continued my perusal of the numerous volumes in the library, and volume 19 drew my attention. It showed the date 1989 on its back, the extraordinary year in which the Berlin Wall was torn down

Peter Jan Margry 2017: Ethnologia Nationum: Or, The World as We See It: "strange, but interesting". *Ethnologia Europaea* 47:1, 30–34. © Museum Tusculanum Press.

and distributed as concrete souvenirs of the obsolete Iron Curtain. Not only for that milestone event, but also in a broader historical perspective, 1989 can, to a certain extent, be perceived as a symbolic fault line in (European) history. The crumbling of the Eastern bloc not only resulted in a reshuffling of states and alliances, it also set in motion a new decade of accelerated Europeanization. The concept and idea of a large, strong, and rich European Union became increasingly taken from outside as a preferred safe haven for migrants coming from outside that new political unity. In later years, the rapid expansion of the Union and creation of open nation-state borders facilitated large-scale East–West migrant movements *within* its territory. Not only parliamentary decisions but also the actions of mobile citizens were transforming Europe into a multicultural political unit.

In a seemingly prescient coincidence, the first issue of that 1989 volume was devoted to the role of nationalism within European culture (Löfgren 1989a). How current could a scholarly journal be? The issue was the result of a Budapest workshop that had been held a year earlier under the title: *National Culture as Process*. Interestingly ethnologists from Sweden and Hungary, across the East–West divide, seemingly already a sign of a softening border, convened there for an interdisciplinary research project on the formation of national cultures. The issue exudes a sort of prophetic topicality, considering the two Germanys at the time were just about to clarify anew their views on the concepts of nation, nationalism, and nationality. German reunification triggered a long-term social, cultural, and political process across the continent that reinvented and reapplied nationalism and national identities, now connected to the process of a rapidly evolving Europeanization (Brubaker 1996).

The issue editor and author of the introductory contribution, entitled "The Nationalization of Culture", was an ethnologist from the Swedish University of Lund, Orvar Löfgren. My colleagues said that he was an interesting and innovative scholar, well worth watching. And so he was. Trained as a medievalist, I found this all to be new and fascinating literature. Löfgren addressed one of the core themes within European ethnology, perhaps *the* core theme in folkloristics' earlier days: the idea of national folk heritages and characters, as part of the formation of nation states and of political and ideological nationalism in Europe (Baycroft & Hopkin 2012). Löfgren and his Swedish and Hungarian colleagues addressed the issues of "national culture" and "national identity" as renewed key concepts relevant for the developments on the continent. Cultural confrontations due to immigration at the local level on the continent began to increase more at the time, and there was much discussion about the nature and remaking of national cultures as a specific cultural tradition and about the threat of the disintegration of such national traditions and identities (Löfgren 1986a) – a threat that had not been discussed and debated for the first time and "probably not the last either…", as Löfgren asserted. From his position as an ethnologist, he called upon the discipline to pay more scholarly attention to the practical everyday organization of cultural loyalty within nationalism instead of the mere politically oriented ideology of nationalism. "What types of cultural meanings and expressions are actually shared on a national level and how do individuals come to share them?" he queried (Löfgren 1986a: 74). Some years earlier, at another colloquy on nationalisms, he had brought up similar preliminary questions. In the mid-1980s, the first large-scale rethink and re-examination of the concepts of national character and national identity were being undertaken (Löfgren 1986b: 112–113). "Nationalism is back" was the simple and obvious observation (Galema, Henkes & Te Velde 1993: 5). Hence, not only in Europe's everyday life or politics, but also within academia, scholars were trying to figure out how nationalism and collective national identities could be better understood. Initial fears of submersion in a generalized European culture, ethnic mixing and shifting boundaries formed the refrain of populist parties and movements (Dundes 1986: 36).[6]

Ideas of an essentialist form of national identity or of a culture as a monolithic concept of the nation – issues often too essentially present within former

Volkskunde – became outdated as seminal works by Benedict Anderson and John Hutchinson transformed the study of nationalism (Anderson 1983; Hutchinson 1987; Leerssen 2006).[7] In particular, Anderson's *Imagined Communities* functioned for ethnologists and cultural historians as a tool for dismantling the static and homogenous house of ideas around nationalism. Löfgren elaborates on this in his article and describes how national culture and identity are in continuous need of deconstruction while simultaneously being in continuous states of reconstruction. However, he warned that this is a fragile construction, one requiring ample reaffirmation in situations of uncertainty and anxiety. Expressions of nationalism, symbolism, or national rhetoric – meant to symbolize the essence of the nation, its inhabitants, or proper norms of national behavior and virtues – form a cultural register of that nation, which, at the same time, work as a strong source of cultural and social identity (Löfgren 1989b: 17–23). It is both fascinating and alarming that we can see all of this happening around us again today. At the time, Löfgren's article made me fully aware of these cultural dimensions and processes related to the re-emergence of the national. It provided me with a state-of-the-art overview, inspiring and relevant for my own work.[8]

Europe's preoccupation with the nation and its people, and the various communities in and outside the Union, has only become stronger. The relatively stable post- (cold) war situation has definitely come to an end. The recent Ukraine-Crimea crisis of 2014 and the refugee crisis of 2015 has made this all the more explicit, all now situated in the political contexts of neo-liberalism, (neo-)nationalism, and populism (Gingrich & Banks 2006). The resurgent myths of nationalism, often cultivated and stimulated through their ideologically and politically construed versions, are blossoming again, taken as the populist new voice. It is an explosive mix and hence a major threat to the Europeanization process, to Europe at large, and subsequently for peace in the whole region. Populist expressions of right-wing nationalism in Russia, Poland, Hungary and Turkey are manifest. Catalan and Scottish independence referenda and a UK choice for "Brexit" in June 2016 are other geopolitical results. These populist measures – which include holding referenda – were described in *The New York Times* as "a battleground for all Western democracies where anti-immigrant hostilities are building" (Nationalism 2016). The two states from which the participants of the 1989 Nationalism workshop hailed are also having their bouts of nationalism. In the center of Europe, Hungary has experienced the self-fulfilling prophecy of the 1989 article on myths and symbols of the past (Sinkó 1989), having broadly embraced an anti-European mentality under the aegis of its ethnocentric president Viktor Orbán. Even immigration-friendly Sweden has become a battleground as a result of this development, which has created fertile ground for patriotism and consciousness of "Swedishness" (Löfgren 1991).[9] And so, an urgent need to research the cultural dimensions, social organization, and ethnic identity of the national still remains.

While local and regional identities are often better researched from an historical perspective (Hobsbawm 1992; Meyer 2003; Jensen 2016), present-day discourses on nationalisms in Europe call for additional research and analysis that need to be presented in the appropriate journals. Some projects have already started.[10] They can build on the foundation laid by Löfgren and associates. As he said in 1989 – and as we can say again today – such projects on nationalism and national culture will "not be the last either". Löfgren made clear that little is known or studied about what is actually shared on a national level and how it is shared. National sharing involves the trivialities of everyday life: the routines and habits of a nation. But these are difficult to describe or articulate. What is visible and what is known to all (Löfgren 1989b: 13–14)? For Löfgren, modern nationalism was like a cultural paradigm: "The national project cannot survive as a mere ideological construction; it must exist as a cultural praxis in everyday life" (Löfgren 1989b: 23). Therefore, the practice of *ethnologia nationum*, the ethnology of nations and nationalism, remains as a thematic field within European ethnology highly important to foster.

I would like to finish this comment again on a personal note. When I was asked to join the executive board of the International Society for Ethnology and Folklore in 2004, one of the first questions I posed to the sitting board, ignorant of its troublesome past, was why *Ethnologia Europaea* was not connected to SIEF. Why was this highly acclaimed academic podium not a SIEF journal? When I suggested to my fellow board members that we should turn *Ethnologia Europaea* into a SIEF journal, they looked away, shrugged their shoulders or cleared their throats. The president then explained to me with a somewhat heavy voice that this was out of the question because of a long and unpleasant history that involved all kinds of delicate and subtle issues that had occurred in the past, related to specific "nationalism" within the field. I got the impression that the situation was seen as a deterministic result of history. Nevertheless, I often wondered and suggested how good it would be to have the journal available for members. Only after more than ten years – I was about to leave the board again – did the journal editors and especially SIEF's current president, unhindered by the past, embrace the idea and successfully push it forward. In 2015, *Ethnologia Europaea* entered into the society as SIEF's flagship journal thus "uniting" the various nationalisms in a scholarly way. A promising win-win situation.

Notes

1 Quote by Orvar Löfgren, from the clip of his ethnological sensation, September 2014: http://www.siefhome.org/videos/ethno_sensations.html.
2 See on this "war": Rogan 2014.
3 On the naming: *Ethnologia Europaea* 44:2, 15, note 5 (2014).
4 Mentioned on the first contents page: Bernet Kempers 1967.
5 He was the first (endowed) professor of European Ethnology at the University of Amsterdam, in the years 1969–1984.
6 Comments given in response to the public discussion held at the colloquy in Nijmegen on "National Character" in April 1985.
7 The idea that all nationalism is cultural nationalism is later further developed by Leerssen 2006, see also his database: http://www.spinnet.eu/cultural-nationalism.
8 For example for my article on one of the major elements of Dutch nationalism, published later in the same journal: Margry 2014.
9 Cf. the popular translations of such concepts: https://sweden.se/culture-traditions/10-youtube-clips-about-swedishness/; cf. Ehn 1989.
10 Ethnologists in München and Amsterdam are independently working on new expressions of nationalism in Europe: http://www.volkskunde.uni-muenchen.de/veranstaltungen/tagungen/neuer-nationalismus/programm-neuer-nationalismus/index.html, accessed October 28, 2016; http://www.meertens.knaw.nl/acee/?page_id=126 (on Dutchness), accessed October 28, 2016.

References

Anderson, Benedict 1983: *Imagined Communities: Reflections on the Origin and Spread of Nationalism*. London: Verso; online: http://rebels-library.org/files/imagined_communities.pdf.

Baycroft, Timothy & David Hopkin (eds.) 2012: *Folklore and Nationalism in Europe during the long Nineteenth Century*. Leiden: Brill.

Bernet Kempers, A.J. 1967: Volkskunde und Universität in den Niederlanden. *Ethnologia Europaea* 1, 278–279.

Brubaker, Rogers 1996: *Nationalism Reframed: Nationhood and the National Question in the New Europe*. Cambridge: Cambridge University Press.

Dundes, Alan 1986: Comments. *Focaal: Tijdschrift voor Antropologie* 1 (April), 36.

Ehn, Billy 1989: National Feeling in Sport: The Case of Sweden. *Ethnologia Europaea* 19, 57–66.

Galema, Annemieke, Barbara Henkes & Henk te Velde (eds.) 1993: *Images of the Nation: Different Meanings of Dutchness, 1870–1940*. Amsterdam: Rodopi, 5.

Gingrich, Andre & Marcus Banks (eds.) 2006: *Neo-Nationalism in Europe and Beyond: Perspectives from Social Anthropology*. New York: Berghahn.

Hobsbawm, Eric J. 1992: *Nations and Nationalism since 1780: Programme, Myth, Reality*. Cambridge: Cambridge University Press, 2nd ed.

Hutchinson, John 1987: *The Dynamics of Cultural Nationalism: The Gaelic Revival and the Creation of the Irish Nation-State*. London: Allen & Unwin.

Jensen, Lotte (ed.) 2016: *The Roots of Nationalism: National Identity Formation in Early Modern Europe, 1600–1815*. Amsterdam: AUP.

Leerssen, Joep 2006: Nationalism and the Cultivation of Culture. *Nations and Nationalism* 12:4, 559–578.

Löfgren, Orvar 1986a: Towards an Anthropology of the National. *Focaal: Tijdschrift voor Antropologie* [later: *Focaal: Journal of Global and Historical Anthropology*] 1 (April), 71–74.

Löfgren, Orvar 1986b: Over de Culturele Organisatie van het National Gevoel: Enkele Overwegingen. *Focaal: Tijdschrift voor Antropologie* 1 (April), 92–116.

Löfgren, Orvar (ed.) 1989a: National Culture as Process. *Ethnologia Europaea* 19, 2–102.
Löfgren, Orvar 1989b: The Nationalization of Culture. *Ethnologia Europaea* 19, 5–24.
Löfgren, Orvar 1991: The Nationalization of Culture: Constructing Swedishness. *Studia Ethnologica Croatica* 3, 101–116.
Margry, Peter Jan 2014: Mobocracy and Monarchy: A Ritualistic Reconciliation with the Anachronism of the Dutch Monarchy. *Ethnologia Europaea* 44:1, 5–22.
Meyer, Silke 2003: *Die Ikonographie der Nation: Nationalstereotype in der englischen Druckgraphik des 18. Jahrhundert.* Münster: Waxmann.
Nationalism and the Brexit Vote. *The New York Times*, June 20, 2016.
Rogan, Bjarne 2014: When the Folklorists Won the Battle but Lost the War: The Cumbersome (Re-)Birth of SIEF in 1964. *Cultural Analysis* 13, 23–50; online: http://socrates.berkeley.edu/~caforum/volume13/pdf/Rogan.pdf.
Sinkó, Katalin 1989: Arpád versus Saint István: Competing Heroes and Competing Interests in the Figurative Representation of Hungarian History. *Ethnologia Europaea* 19, 67–84.

Peter Jan Margry is an ethnologist and historian who works at the Meertens Institute in Amsterdam. He holds a chair of European Ethnology at the University of Amsterdam. His research interests involve religious cultures, memorialization, rituality and heritage. His latest publication is *Spiritualizing the City: Agency and Resilience of the Urban and Urbanesque Habitat* (Milton Park: Routledge, 2017), a volume co-edited with Victoria Hegner.
(peterjan.margry@meertens.knaw.nl)

THE NATIONALIZATION OF CULTURE

Reprinted from *Ethnologia Europaea* 19:1, 1989

Orvar Löfgren

Although nationalism is an example of a cultural force which in many cases has overruled other, traditional identities and loyalties in nineteenth- and twentieth-century society, the study of nationalism has not been focused very much on the cultural praxis of national identity formation and sharing. As a result, the ideology and politics of nationalism are far better understood than the creation of Hungarianness and Swedishness.

This paper[1] discusses some approaches in the national culture-building of everyday life, using mainly Swedish examples. The focus is also on national culture as a battle arena, where different interest groups use arguments about national unity or heritage in hegemonic struggles.

Different types of "nationalization processes" are discussed, as for example ways in which certain cultural domains come to be defined as national, how national space is transformed into cultural space, or the way in which every new generation not only is nationalized into a given heritage but also creates its own version of a common, national frame of reference.

Keywords: national-culture building, national identity, everyday-life nationalisation, historical anthropology, comparative approach, Sweden

Revisiting the National Project

Nationalism is of special interest to that branch of anthropology within which most of the following essays were produced: European ethnology, a discipline born in the nineteenth century as a child of nationalism and Herder's *Volksgeist*. European ethnology and folklore developed with the more or less explicit goal of salvaging and assembling "national" folk cultures. This strongly ideologically charged project also included ideas about folk mentalities or national character.

Later generations of ethnologists faced the task of critically deconstructing these pioneer attempts at creating a national folk heritage, and it is only after such a purge that it has become possible to return to the question of national identity and culture with new theoretical perspectives.

This collection of papers was born out of this recent ethnological interest in new perspectives on the making and remaking of national cultures. The starting point was a collaboration between researchers in Sweden and Hungary. In Budapest Tamás Hofer had, together with a group of colleagues, analysed the construction of a Hungarian national identity and the crucial role of folk culture in this pro-

Orvar Löfgren 2017: The Nationalization of Culture. Reprinted from 1989 *Ethnologia Europaea* 19:1, 5–24.
Ethnologia Europaea 47:1, 35–53. © Museum Tusculanum Press.

cess, in Stockholm Åke Daun and Billy Ehn, among others, had been studying Swedish mentalities and changing self-representations, especially in the light of the recent waves of immigration to Sweden (cf. Daun & Ehn 1988). In Lund a group including Jonas Frykman and myself had worked on a project concerning class formation and culture-building in nineteenth- and twentieth-century Sweden, where one of our main tasks was to scrutinize ideas about a modern and homogeneous Swedish national culture and to look at the extent to which clichés and notions of national homogeneity concealed a cultural differentiation based upon factors like class, gender and generations (see Löfgren 1986).

These various approaches of deconstructing and reconstructing national culture-building had led all of us towards an interest both in the ways in which *national rhetoric* had been used as an argument in hegemonic conflicts between competing interests and classes in Hungarian and Swedish society during the last century (Do some Hungarian/Swedes claim to be more Hungarian/Swedish than others?), but also in the question of how behind this ideological facade of national unity, an *actual* nationalization of shared cultural understandings and knowledge had been established. To what extent, for example, do Swedes or Hungarians of today share a common frame of reference compared with the situation fifty or a hundred years ago?

It became evident that the cultural politics of nation building and the process of nationalizing culture are best studied within a comparative framework, in order not to be blocked by the occupational disease always threatening scholars looking at their native culture: what we in Sweden call "home-blindness".

This collection of essays is the first result of a joint discussion of Hungarian and Swedish research into the making and remaking of national cultures.[2]

Åke Daun's contribution, "Studying national culture by means of quantitative methods" mainly deals with the methodological problems of studying contemporary culture on a national level combining qualitative and quantitative approaches. Drawing from an ongoing research project he discusses various strategies for locating basic themes and personality traits on a national level, trying to avoid the pitfalls of earlier grandiose speculations about "national character".

Jonas Frykman's paper "Social mobility and national character" looks at ideas about what is seen as "typically Swedish" and relates them to the culture-building of Swedish intellectuals in the making of the modern welfare state. It is their style of life and outlook on the world that has often been expressed in terms of "national character". He analyses the social and cultural conditions under which such images of culture and personality are produced – a society with a high degree of mobility.

His analysis of a national setting, where progressive intellectuals have dominated the discourse on national culture and "Swedishness" can be compared to Peter Niedermüller's paper on class and national culture in Hungary, "Symbols and reality in national culture: The Hungarian case". Here the cultural battle over who represents the true Hungarian identity has been carried out within a very different social structure. He discusses the various paths developed in attempts to construct a Hungarian identity and heritage through uses of folk culture and the competing interests involved in these processes.

A neglected field of study is the strong modern connection between sport and nationalism. In his paper, "National feeling in sport", Billy Ehn discusses the national rhetorics of sport and the ways in which they express national sentiments and loyalties, using material mainly from Swedish sport journalism.

Katalin Sinkó's paper "Árpád versus Saint István: Competing interests in the figurative representation of Hungarian history" looks at processes of confrontation and negotiation between competing national heroes, symbolizing two different sets of ideas about Hungary and Hungarianness, which have been used by different groups for different purposes over the centuries.

Lena Johannesson discusses a different genre of figurative representations in her paper "Anti-heroic heroes in more or less heroic media". She looks at the ways in which Swedish anti-heroes have been portrayed in twentieth-century media and the ways in which these national images are comments on "Swedish" virtues and vices.

Food seems to have a magic position in the maintenance of a national identity among expatriates, who long to feel the tastes of the old country. Lists of what is "typical" Swedish often include food items. In her paper, "From peasant dish to national symbol: An early deliberate example", Eszter Kisbán traces a very marked Hungarian example of the making of a national dish and the ways in which this Hungarian symbol has been used in cultural politics as well as in the tourist industry marketing of Hungarian culture.

New Dialogues

The scope of the papers indicates the new kind of interdisciplinary dialogues developed in the field of study of national culture and identity. For a long time this kind of dialogue was poorly developed. Although there were some attempts at cross-disciplinary exchanges, a fairly conventional division of labour existed, in which historians concentrated on nationalism as a political and ideological phenomenon, whereas anthropologists mainly worked within the conceptual framework of ethnicity, mostly with an emphasis on synchronic perspectives. This traditional division is, however, slowly disintegrating, as historians become more interested in nations as cultural formations and anthropologists have begun to interest themselves in the cultural politics of nation-building.[3]

Up till a few years ago research on national identity was to a great extent focused on the ideology and politics of nationalism, often within a framework of exposing nationalism as a type of false consciousness. There were so many myths of national culture, so much ideological rhetoric waiting to be scrutinized and exposed. (A fairly typical example of this genre is Ernest Gellner's book *Nations and Nationalism* from 1983.) This was a necessary phase of research which now enables us to look in a more detached way at nationalism as a cultural phenomenon and as a historical process. (See, for example, the much more nuanced approach found in Benedict Anderson's influential discussion of the origins and spread of nationalism from 1983.)

In spite of the expanding literature we still live with an underdeveloped and ambiguous analytical framework, as Philip Schlesinger has pointed out in his critical survey of current research (1987); concepts like national identity, culture, mentality or heritage are still vaguely defined.

Being National?

When entering the Nordic Museum, a nineteenth-century child of Swedish nationalism, you first encounter the imposing statue of the Swedish king Gustav Vasa, often seen as the sixteenth-century founder of the Swedish nation state. Under his stern gaze is a carved motto directed to the visitor: "Be Ye Swedish!" (*Warer Swenske!*)

This early twentieth-century version of a royal command may illustrate the first analytical problem, that of working with concepts which cannot easily be moved around in history. An adjective like "national" or "Swedish" has totally different connotations for different epochs and different social groups. The twentieth-century message of the importance of being Swedish would have made very little sense to Gustav Vasa's peasant subjects. Swedishness is a quality which can hardly be used trans-historically, at least not without a discussion of how this elusive trait is defined or redefined in different historical settings.

In the same way we have an extensive debate on the concept of nationalism. Should it be reserved for the ideological and political movements from the late eighteenth century onwards, as a product of the intellectual climate of the American and French revolutions? Is it possible or meaningful to talk about nationalism in medieval England or sixteenth-century Sweden? It seems to me reasonable to make an analytical distinction between the concepts of *patriotism* and *nationalism* in this comparative context, as representing two different cultural paradigms in nation-building. The wider concept of patriotism is based upon the love of God, King and Country by *subjects* of the state, whereas the idea of nationalism is based upon ideas about a "Volksgemeinschaft", a shared history and culture, a common destiny, an idea of equality and fellowship, which means that nationalism contains political dynamite and can thus be used both to mask class interests or to fight them.

A middle-class family on the beach with the Swedish flag hoisted on the top of the tent, photo from the 1920s. Private flags were then still a rather exotic sight, or as a rural answer to a questionnaire on the use of this national symbol put it in 1940: "In my childhood towards the end of the nineteenth century the Swedish flag was an almost unknown concept. It was a good bit later into the next century that I started to see the blue and yellow flag among upper-class types and in vicarages... Hardly anybody thought of the flag as a symbol of the nation but rather as something tied to royalty, militarism and well-to-do people. The result was that the flag did not become popular among the less well-to-do and it still isn't, because the tradition is tenacious" (quoted after Biörnstad 1976: 48).

On the whole the national flag became a popular symbol rather late in Sweden. Brave attempts were made to create a national holiday, called "The day of the Swedish flag" from 1916, but this national celebration has remained a rather empty, official ritual with none of the popular fervour of the fourth or the fourteenth of July.

Interestingly enough, while official flag-waving is rather limited (and often joked about) in the Scandinavian countries, the private use of national flags is today more common here than anywhere else in the world. Flagpoles are found everywhere, next to summer houses, in caravan camps as well as in suburban gardens, and the flag is hoisted on all kinds of occasions, from family birthdays to Midsummer parties.

In the following I concentrate on the period of the nineteenth and twentieth centuries: the grand centuries of nationalist ideology and nation states as opposed to the earlier era of the absolute monarchies. I will mainly focus on the problem of the making and constant remaking of national identity and culture, as an arena of contestation between different interests.

Do-It-Yourself Nationalism?

The National Flag, the National Anthem and the National Emblem are the three symbols through which an independent country proclaims its identity and sovereignty and, as such, they command instantaneous respect and loyalty. In themselves they reflect the entire background, thought and culture of a nation. (After Firth 1973: 314)

This quote from a pamphlet published by the Indian Government in the 1960s illustrates the ways in which a common symbolic language of nationhood is taken for granted today.

The interesting paradox in the emergence of nationalism is that it is an international ideology which is imported for national ends. Looking back at the pioneer era of Western national culture-building we may view this ideology of nationalism as a gigantic do-it-yourself kit. Gradually a set of ideas is developed as to what elements make up a proper nation, the ingredients which are needed to turn state formations into national cultures with a shared symbolic capital. The experiences and strategies of creating national languages, heritages and symbolic estates etc., are circulated among intellectual activists in different corners of the world and the eventual result is a kind of check-list: every nation should have not only a common language, a common past and destiny, but also a national folk culture, a national character or mentality, national values, perhaps even some national tastes and a national landscape (often enshrined in the form of national parks), a gallery of national myths and heroes (and villains), a set of symbols, including flag and anthem, sacred texts and images, etc. This national inventory is produced mainly during the nineteenth century, but elaborated during the twentieth.

The process in which national projects are made *trans*national, and recycled or remade in different settings and at different times is still with us, as new nations continue to be born within the same basic nineteenth-century paradigm. It is thus an irony that the liberating force of nationalism in developing countries can be seen in a way as the ultimate victory of colonial hegemony, as the nation-building is often carried out along truly Western lines.

The late-comers to this process of nation-building also have to live with the ironic comments of the pioneers. For the latter their own national identity has had time to be transformed from an ideological construction to a given, natural fact, and in their ridiculing of late-comers' attempts to create national symbols (mainly in the Third World) the "old" nations fail to see the parallels to their own past. Ernest Gellner has touched on this problem which is sometimes boiled down to the derogative maxim "I am a patriot, he is a nationalist and they are tribalists" (Gellner 1983: 87).

Constructing National Identity

Gellner's quote underlines the fact that some national ideologies have been naturalized so early that they are rarely questioned today. Norbert Elias has pointed at the same problem in his comparison of French and German self-representations:

> The questions "What is really French? What is really English?" have long since ceased to be a matter of much discussion for the French and English. But for centuries "What is really German?" had not been laid to rest. (Elias [1939]1978: 6)

If there is a certain chameleonic vagueness about the concept of nationalism, it is still usually contained within the field of meanings denoting ideology, doctrine or political movement. The use of the concept of *national identity* is, however, more ambivalent, and it is probably in the development of this concept that ethnicity theory can make its most fruitful contribution, namely in the focus on identity as a dynamic process of construction and reproduction over time, in direct relation or opposition to specific other groups and interests: it is this dynamic and dialectical approach to identity management that is important here (cf. Schlesinger 1987).

During the last decade ethnicity studies have stressed the ways in which ethnic boundaries may change over time, how ethnic markers and symbols are created and communicated and how different criteria of identity can be selected in different situations. (There is, of course, the risk that this focus on the strategic aspects of ethnicity management overstates the fluidity, malleability and manipulatory aspects of ethnic identity.)

National identity can thus be seen as a specific form of collective identity. Like ethnic identity, it can be both latent and manifest: activated in special situations, confrontations or settings, dormant in others.

In what ways are national identities different from ethnic ones, and not only a specific variation on the ethnicity theme? It is evident that a force like nationalism often uses ethnicity as a basis for constructing national cultures, but it can also be argued (in some cases) that an ethnic identity can be a by-product of nation-building. National identity can also be superimposed on traditional ethnic cleavages, turning Finns and Swedes into fellow countrymen in Finland, or producing true Americans out of a mosaic of immigrants. We need to devote more attention to the ways in which national identity in a gradual process comes to transcend and subordinate other loyalties, be they regional, ethnic, or based upon class, gender or religion. How is it that national identity often works so well as an *inclusive* symbol?

Unlike ethnic identities national ones are always directly linked to problems of state formation and state discourse. They are produced and reproduced within a very special institutional framework, which

Towards the end of the nineteenth century the northern province of Dalecarlia came to be seen as the typical Swedish peasant heritage. Urban intellectuals made pilgrimages to this rather atypical piece of Sweden, where peasants still wore folk costumes, lived in large villages and maintained colourful rituals. "Dalecarlia with its solid people, its cottages, its old traditions, which still survive up here… where everything speaks *Swedish* as in no other region, and nowhere else does one feel so happy and proud of being Swedish as there," exclaimed one of the visitors in 1899 (quoted in Rosander 1987: 315).

The reason that Dalecarlia was chosen as the cradle of Sweden was not only the picturesque peasant life still surviving in the region but also because Dalecarlian culture fitted the middle-class mythology of "the old peasant society". There was no large rural proletariat to disturb the image of a happy village *Gemeinschaft*, and here one found the stereotypes of a freedom-loving, individualistic, and principled peasantry, embodying honesty, honour and love of traditions, living a simple life in close contact with nature. In short, the Dalecarlians represented the kind of cultural ancestors the new progressive middle-class intelligentsia wanted to have.

It is therefore no coincidence that the first building brought to the new open air museum Skansen in Stockholm (opened in 1891) was taken from Dalecarlia. Outside the cottage, museum guides pose in the Dalecarlian dresses, which were later developed into something of a national folk costume for the urban middle class. (Photo: The Nordic Museum) sets them apart from other types of identity constructs.

Benedict Anderson has discussed national identity in terms of "imagined communities" of national fellowship. His by now almost classic definition of the nation runs:

> It is an imagined political community and imagined as both inherently limited and sovereign.
>
> It is imagined because the members of even the smallest nation will never know most of their fellow-members, meet them or even hear of them, yet in the minds of each lives the image of their communion. (Anderson 1983: 15)

In a discussion of Anderson's thesis Michael Harbsmeier has argued that his use of the anthropologist Victor Turner's *communitas* concept is too broad, it does not help us to understand the very specific nature of "the national community", as opposed to the *communitas* of religious groups or empires. He develops Anderson's framework by arguing that national identity is, unlike many other forms of social identity, totally dependent upon the imagined or real approval of this identity as a national otherness by others, that is, other nations (Harbsmeier 1986: 52).

The fact that national identity is always defined as a contrast or a complement to other nations, is illustrated by the nineteenth-century Scandinavian national movements. Norwegian nationalism was born, not in Norway, but among Norwegian students and intellectuals in Copenhagen towards the end of the eighteenth century. The Norwegian national identity came to be profiled against the centuries of Danish rule and the enforced union with Sweden from 1814. It is no coincidence that it was the historical period of up to 1300, before the union with Denmark, that came into focus in the creation of a Norwegian cultural heritage: Norwegians were above all Vikings (cf. Østerud 1987). In the Finnish national movement, folklore became even more important. The search for a Finnish folk literature and the emphasis on Finnish as a national language was a counter to the former Swedish domination and the new Russian rule after 1809. This construction of a national Finnish folk culture was a task mainly carried out by the Swedish-speaking intellectual elite, who in this process had to become even more Finnish than the peasantry itself (cf. Honko 1980).

In nineteenth-century Denmark the construction of a national heritage and a national identity was above all profiled against the arch-enemy in the south, Germany, while Swedish nationalism of this era really lacked an arch-enemy or rather the threat of a dominating neighbour, as the traditional fear of Russian intervention had diminished. Against this background it is hardly surprising that the cult of *Scandinavianism* became a Swedish speciality, or even a kind of substitute nationalism. The national anthem talks about the "mountainous North" and the national folk museum was named the "Nordic Museum".

Without analysing this national culture building as a *contrasting* project we cannot explain the different strategic uses made, for example, of folk culture in the nineteenth-century Scandinavian context. It is no coincidence that the authentic Norwegian peasant was to be found in the remote mountain valleys of Telemark and his Swedish counterpart in Dalecarlia, or that true Finnish folk culture survived in the forests of Karelia.[4]

For Hungary Tamás Hofer has analysed a similar process of stereotyping (see Hofer n.d.). The Hungarian peasant of the plains was created as a national contrast to the Austrian mountain peasant. Hofer has also discussed the ways in which a national peasant folk culture was used by different groups for hegemonic ends at different points in Hungarian history – for example, the elaborate use of folk culture as national symbolism during the Stalinist era of the 1950s. This was the great period for "state folklorism" in Eastern Europe, when smiling factory girls paraded in peasant costumes and the image of the "traditional folk" was used in appeals for national unity by the new rulers. Today, as Eszter Kisbán points out in her paper, the tourist industry is one of the chief marketing agencies for such stereotypes of national folklore.

The anthropologist Michael Herzfeld has explored the cultural politics of folklore in his studies of the remaking of a Greek national identity after the end of Turkish rule in the nineteenth century, a process in which the Greek cultural heritage had to be purified of all Eastern elements and appear in a manner which conformed to European stereotypes of the true, classical Greek nation (see Herzfeld 1987).

Even the American immigrant nation developed a search for its own "folk culture" at the beginning of the twentieth century, when collectors and scholars roamed the Appalachian mountains in search of an "Elizabethan culture" whose bearers spoke like Shakespeare and plaited baskets while singing medieval ballads. This traditional culture had to be salvaged and reproduced in order to stem the disintegrating forces both from the modern world and the new waves of proletarian immigrants (Whisnant 1983).

Examples like these illustrate the ways in which folk culture becomes nationalized (and also sacralised). A correct, authorized and timeless version of folk life is produced through the processes of selection, categorization, relocation and "freezing". One of the most interesting parts of this process is what is *left out*, (more or less unconsciously) disregarded or ignored as not being worthy of entering the showcases of the new national museums or the pages of the folklore heritage publications.

It is, however, important not to reduce these processes of the nationalization of folk culture to one of just "inventing traditions". Here we have a much more complex pattern of accommodation, reorganization and recycling, in which different interest groups have different claims at stake. (Cf. the discussion of the ways in which Swedish and Hungarian intellectuals used the folk culture as a strategy of cultural politics in the contributions below by Niedermüller, Sinkó, and Frykman.)

If national peasants were produced in contrast to competing national images of other nations, the same process of profiling is found in the creation of national stereotypes: the typical Swede or Hungarian is usually profiled (consciously or unconsciously) against a counterpart and it is interesting to note that the stereotype tends to change with the object of comparison.

In relation to the happy-go-lucky nations of the Mediterranean, Swedes define themselves as grey and boring, obsessed with order, punctuality and the control of emotions, characterized by a total lack of spontaneity and *esprit-de-vie*. If the comparison is made in relation to Finns or Russians, other qualities are stressed, because these Northern neighbours are often stereotyped as even greyer and more boring: they even make the Swedes look a little bohemian. On the whole there is an interesting metaphor of North and South in national self-representation: one's own identity is contrasted with those who are more Southern and easy-going (but less dependable) and those who are Northerners and less easy-going than one's fellow countrymen. There seems to be a tendency in many settings to produce an image which is based upon an idea of the golden mean. "We English are not as warm and hot-tempered as the French or the Spaniards, but more dependable and efficient; on the other hand, we are not as rigid or controlled as the Germans or the Scandinavians."[5] Ideas about emotional control or lack of it seem very central in these kinds of stereotypes, where North and South often stand for the cultural opposition of cold and warm. Another striking feature of these stereotypes is their gender bias. Although *das Vaterland* is usually symbolized by a national mother – Britannia, Marianne, Mother Denmark and Mother Svea (of Sweden) – the typical Swede, Dane or German is usually a man.

But national stereotypes also reflect changing geopolitical conditions, as for example in the altered ways in which Hungarians have viewed the Austrians, from the period of Habsburgian dominance to the contemporary situation, or the manners in which Danes have defined Swedes over the last century (and vice-versa). There is always an element of underdog–topdog argumentation in the ways national pride or national identity are expressed in relation to neighbourhood nations, be they defined as Big Brothers or Little Sisters.[6]

To conclude, one may argue that the construction of national identity is a task which calls for internal and external communication. In order to create a symbolic community, identity markers have to be created *within* the national arena in order to achieve a sense of belonging and loyalty to the national project, but this identity also has to be marketed to the outside world as a national otherness. Such projects of self-presentation and self-definition can be analysed in many cultural arenas during the nineteenth and twentieth centuries. (An example of the latter is the big world exhibitions from 1851 and onwards, where nations have peddled their self-images; cf. the discussion in Benedict 1983, Rydell 1984 and Smeds 1983.)

National Culture

National identity and national culture are often used as interchangeable concepts. Here I would like to argue for the need to keep them apart, reserving the concept of national culture for that kind of collective sharing which exists on a national level or within a national cultural space. Rather little research in this field has studied *what* is actually shared on a national level and *how* it is shared.

It is quite clear that communication is a crucial problem here: how are these imagined communities shaped and held together over time, how is the social and political space of the nation also transformed into a *cultural* space: a common culture? This sharing is done in different ways and on different levels.

Let us think about the various ingredients which may be contained in the vague concept of national culture. First of all, I think we have to distinguish between "The National Culture" and an everyday national sharing of memories, symbols and knowledge. "The National Culture" which the French historian Maurice Agulhon (1987) has also termed "The national school culture" (or *la Grande Culture*) is a normative cultural capital: What Every Frenchman Should Know. This is the kind of knowledge which is dished out in school, carrying the authorized seal of the official public culture. The making of this kind of normative cultural heritage is an interesting study in itself. The boundaries between ideas about what every Swede *ought* to know and what all Swedes *actually* share tend, however, to become rather blurred.

An interesting example of this confusion of a descriptive and normative approach to national culture is found in the recent study *Cultural Literacy: What Every American Needs to Know* (Hirsch 1987). Hirsch starts out by trying to delineate what actually is shared on a national level, using the USA as his case:

> Suppose we think of American public culture as existing in three segments. At one end is our *civil religion*, which is laden with definitive value traditions. Here we have absolute commitments to freedom, patriotism, equality, self-government, and so on. At the other end of the spectrum is the *vocabulary* of our national discourse, by no means empty of content but nonetheless value-neutral in the sense that it is used to support all the conflicting values that arise in public discourse... Between these two extremes lies the vast middle domain of culture proper. Here are the concrete politics, customs, technologies, and legends that define and determine our current attitudes and actions and our institutions. Here we find constant change, growth, conflict. This realm determines the texture of our national life. (Hirsch 1987: 102)

Hirsch's categorization can be questioned, but his aim is to look at the domain of vocabulary, or rather what he terms *the cultural literacy* of a given nation: "the whole system of widely shared information and associations" (1987: 103), the kind of cultural competence needed to be able to take part in public discourse. Where he goes wrong is in his insistence that this national cultural capital belongs to a general mainstream culture which stands above class interests and power relations. The problem of hegemony and contestation is brushed away and his ultimate aim, thus, becomes rather futile, namely a list of 4,500 dates, places, people, events, books, phrases and sayings that make up the American common culture.

This attempt at standardization mirrors a given social position, reflecting the perspective of a middle-class, middle-aged WASP. The whole project again illustrates the difficulty of separating normative and descriptive approaches to what constitutes a national culture or shared knowledge.

Let me illustrate this dilemma further by quoting a couple of less ambitious attempts at defining national sharing. First T.S. Eliot's classical list of English institutions:

> Derby-day, the Henley regatta, Cowes, August the 12th, a cup final, the greyhound races, the Fortuna game, the dart board, Wensleydale cheese, cabbage boiled in cloves, pickled beetroots, churches in nineteenth-century Gothic and Elgar's music. (Eliot 1949: 30)

Here is a Swedish version from 1985:

> To be Swedish is to have experienced the Swedish summer in all its glory, it is Christmas morning, it is the high school graduation. It is to have been dressed up for the last day of school and to have seen the sun set over the edge of the forest, it is to have lit the Advent candles and to have read Elsa Beskow and seen the king. It is to have walked across a barrack square and to have stood by a grave. (Nordstedt 1985)

Both these examples are an insider's list of cultural traits, made for other insiders. They are lists of key symbols or key events which probably have a rich field of cultural connotations and evoke shared memories of similar situations. They both claim to have captured the *essence* or spirit of Englishness or Swedishness, but they reflect *one* version of or perspective on what constitutes the typical or essential in the national culture. This is England and Sweden described through the cultural lenses of two (male) intellectuals.

If we ask other persons to make up lists like these, we will get a wide range of variations with some common focus, but above all there is a tendency for people to pick very *visible* national traits: public rituals, family feasts, favourite dishes, key symbols and images. It is the "Sunday Best" version of the national culture which is often described, and it is interesting

The patterns of national sharing are also demonstrated in images and visual clichés which became saturated with symbolic meaning. This process of cultural condensation is very marked in the development of national sceneries. One of the best Swedish examples of this is the view of the little red cottage in the meadow at the edge of the lake, a landscape reproduced on scores of postcards and travel brochures. This image evokes a range of associations and connotations, which may produce profound homesickness or ironic comments – reactions which are hard for the outsider to grasp.

to reflect upon how such symbolic compressions of national culture are created and changed over time. You will hardly get the same list in 1920 as in 1988. Eliot's use of Elgar can be taken as one example of this gradual selection. In 1972 another fellow countryman states that "Elgar is loved by the English people as one of the greatest English composers and also for his unique expression of the deep intangible feelings of England" (quoted after Crump 1986: 164).

But as Jeremy Crump has shown in his analysis of the reception of Elgar, his music gradually became defined as typically English through being performed on ceremonial occasions and also by being put to patriotic use during the First World War.

The selection of items for such "Top Ten" lists of national symbols will often include small details or seemingly trivial elements, which are symbolic representations or distillations of central ideas or patterns of behaviour. They have, as Billy Ehn has put it, "a high specific cultural weight". He points out that images of Swedishness can be evoked in memories of the tastes and smells emanating from the traditional midsummer meal of pickled herring, new potatoes and cold aquavit: "a phenomenon which mirrors a whole cultural universe, images of summer, festivity, pleasure and nationhood" (Ehn 1983: 14).

The impact of such events depends not only on their being very visible rituals, but also on their sensual or emotional quality. The common national memories and understandings are sometimes more strongly articulated in non-verbal forms, in shared smells, sounds, tastes and visions. Raymond Williams has coined the concept *structure of feelings* for such elusive cultural phenomena, which cannot be described in terms of ideology or worldview (Williams 1977). In this sense, some feelings are more national than others, that is, they have a stronger symbolic charge.

I would, however, argue that the most important aspects of this national sharing are anchored in the trivialities of everyday life, in the ways in which we can talk about Swedish routines and habits. These traits are so obvious to us that we do not even consider them as typically Swedish. They are easier for an outsider to observe. Concepts like Swedishness and Englishness, for example, imply that there is a certain cultural praxis as well as style that is contained within the national boundaries.

It is interesting to think about what people actually mean when they talk about a person behaving in a "very Swedish" way or looking "very British". People often find it difficult to actually verbalize these traits: they will say vaguely that there is something very Swedish about the way he carries his body, eats his meal, expresses certain feelings or laughs at a joke. Intangible traits like this make up one elusive part of a national cultural capital, or rather – to continue with Bourdieu's terminology – a national habitus or a set of dispositions. When people talk about Swedishness, they talk about this kind of imponderabilia, rather than about "cultural heritage" or *la Grande Culture*. Swedishness then denotes not so much what people talk about but their way of talking: the styles in which a problem is addressed, an argument carried on or a conflict resolved (or suppressed).

To conclude: a concept like national culture is in acute need of deconstruction: what kinds of knowledge of shared understandings is this national capital made up of, which parts of this capital are highly visible, which forms are less articulated or tangible? Are we talking about what all Swedes know or what they ought to know? It seems important to distinguish between, on the one hand, the symbolic capital that is defined as national and patriotic and, on the other hand, the knowledge and experiences which happen to be contained within national boundaries: the inside jokes, associations, references and memories which Swedes understand and Norwegians don't. In short, how can we categorize these different forms of sharing into registers or levels of a "national culture"?

How Wide is Nation-Wide?

The problem of sharing raises questions of communication and the creation of national arenas of interaction. The making of a nation is thus a problem very much linked to the project of *integration* and *standardization*. Language is a good example of this. One of the early aims of nationalists was to create a national language, often in settings where the spoken or written word did not respect national boundaries. For nineteenth-century Norwegian nationalists the creation of a truly Norwegian standard language meant that old influences from written Danish had to be contested, but also that the border between Norway and Sweden had to be made into a linguistic boundary as well, in spite of the fact that people on both sides of that border shared a common dialect. The task of the linguists was to create a standard Norwegian language and the job of the school system was to make sure all Norwegians learned to speak it (cf. Österud 1986: 13). All over Europe we can study the same process, which also led to the creation of specific academic disciplines and school subjects, like "Swedish", "Danish" or "English". (See the discussion of the Scandinavian case in Teleman 1986 and for Britain, Coils & Dodd 1986.)

If language became an important medium for national cohesion and belonging (in most, but far from all nations), the nationalization of culture was very much linked to the creation of *a public sphere* by the rising bourgeoisie, who created new arenas and media of debate and information. We need to study the ways in which this kind of public discourse was turned into a *national* discourse.

Benedict Anderson has argued for the importance of what he calls "print capitalism" in producing a national community. He focuses on the role of the new media of newspapers in the late eighteenth and nineteenth centuries and their role in supplying intellectuals with a forum for national exchanges. In Sweden it is evident that the creation of a multitude of local newspapers had this cohesive effect, in spite of the fact that there was no "national" paper in the nineteenth century (although there were some magazines). There was a constant borrowing and recycling of material between papers and a debate which made the local doctor or bureaucrat out in the province feel that he was taking part in a national discourse and had a knowledge of what was happening in the national capital.

Another new mass medium was the national school book. In Sweden the standard reader for the elementary school (*Folkskolans läsebok*) was used in all Swedish schools from 1868 up to around 1900. Several generations of Swedes, thus, grew up reading the same texts and looking at the same pictures (Furuland 1987).

Media like these not only created national communities of communication but also produced gaps or communicative barriers between, for example, Swedes and Danes. Cultural sharing in a sense became less regional and more national but also less international during the nineteenth century. The Swedish elite talked and read more Swedish and less French and Latin, while the peasants were drawn into a national framework of thought and action.

During the twentieth century the mass media have often been seen as the symbol (or scapegoat) of the *internationalization* of national cultures, but even in the age of satellite television and rock videos I would argue for a more differentiated analysis of this phenomenon. The new media of our century, like radio and television, have played a crucial role in a further nationalization of culture. Many of the nineteenth-century media still remained class-based media, and a truly national public discourse was not created until the twentieth century.

In two other studies (Löfgren 1989 and n.d.) I have looked at this kind of massmediation of national culture: first in the ways in which a "national nature" is created in nineteenth-century Sweden – a set of sceneries which most Swedes learn to recognize as "typically Swedish", views packed with national symbolism. This process of framing and condensing national messages in a piece of nature cannot be understood without reference to the mass-production of landscape sceneries, from oleographs to picture postcards and travel brochures and this production of national images was also helped by the proliferation of texts and songs about Swedish nature.

The other example looks at the very crucial role of radio broadcasting in establishing a national sharing. I have tentatively argued that the period of national broadcasting (and later television) with a one-channel system between about 1930 and 1970 has had an enormous integrating effect in Swedish culture and everyday life. These were decades when (almost) all Swedes listened to the same radio programmes or later viewed the same TV-shows.

In the late 1920s and the 1930s national broadcasting gave Swedes a common focus, common topics of conversation and frames of references. A new kind of imagined community was developed as Swedes all over the country listened in to the same media event, be it the Sunday service, a sports transmission or a popular cabaret. New national personalities were created and even the weather was nationalized in the magic chanting of temperatures and winds from meteorological stations all over the country. National broadcasting also created a national rhythm of listening. People flocked to the morning gymnastics, waited eagerly for the gramophone hour, gathered for the evening news and went to bed with the national anthem, which ended each broadcasting day. The radio created new national traditions, such as the New Year's Eve celebrations. At midnight a mighty community of listeners stood to attention as the church bells from all Swedish cathedrals rang in a new Swedish year.

But even today, with a much more pluralistic media world, we must look at the ways in which international influences are nationalized into a local context as they cross the border. Dallas, Disney and Dynasty have different meanings and play different roles in different national settings. Sweden is, for example, often presented as the most Americanized country in Europe, but this Americanization has been carried out in an extremely Swedish manner. For a visitor from the USA it is often hard to recognize this American influence in the Swedish way of life: there is what Robert Redfield once termed an interesting process of *parochialization* going on in Stockholm as well as in Budapest. Ulf Hannerz has developed the concept of *creolization* for this local transformation of cultural flows within the world system in a discussion of American culture (Hannerz 1987).

A good example of the effect of national cultural barriers is found in the international world of advertising, where it is often demonstrated that an American or French advertisement cannot simply be transplanted into a Swedish magazine – it needs to be reworked by a local agency.

In the same way, consumer culture may also be both an internationalizing and a nationalizing force. One of the really strong cohesive national forces in the United States is to be found in consumer patterns and messages (cf. for example Roland Marchand's study *Advertising the American Dream*, 1985). Consumption in the USA is in a way very American, with brands, styles and habits which keep the 50 states together, but also create barriers to the outside world. These barriers are often demonstrated in the popular jokes about American tourist complaints about the lack American ways (especially foodways) in foreign countries. The establishment of a number of national chains of shops, motels, restaurants and other commercial institutions has created a standardized pattern which makes the Californian feel at home in both Idaho and South Carolina. (When the waitress approaches him in such distant territories asking what kind of salad dressing he would prefer with his meal, he instantly knows that there are three choices: French, Blue cheese or Thousand Island.)

To conclude: we need to develop a study of nationalizing media, agents, institutions and arenas. How is the nation established as a *nationwide* cultural space, as a horizon or communicative community, and how is the boundary towards other nations maintained? Such an analysis must focus on everything from schools and national (military) service to TV commercials and fashions, and it must examine the way regional or subcultural worlds are made national and the way international messages are creolized.

The Disintegrating Nation

Another perspective on this communicative process is found in the discourse on the disintegrating national culture, a discourse which is at least as old as nationalism itself. Nations have always been seen as falling apart, but the forces (or threats) of disintegration tend to vary through time.

One constant threat has been defined as regionalism, but this concept covers a wide range of relations, which may fluctuate in interesting ways from nation to nation and from time to time. France is a good example of highly varied regional movements, changing not only in focus and intensity but also in their political profile during the last two centuries.

Many forms of regionalism may function not as a potential threat to national break-up but rather as a

In 1909 a prize competition for a Swedish national monument was launched. A private donator had written to the king and pointed out that Sweden still lacked such a manifestation, which could demonstrate the Swedish people's gratitude for its country, state and culture and also create a feeling of national unity.

Of the 36 contributions, the only one remembered today is Sven Boberg's "Sleep in peace", with Mother Sweden snoring on the throne, flanked by the two heroes king Gustavus Adolphus and Charles the XII, who are squeezed into their boots. The artist suggested that his statue should be positioned in the entrance to the Houses of Parliament, in order to make sure that no one could get in or out.

A national monument was never erected in Sweden. 1909 was certainly not the right moment, as the nation witnessed the biggest general strike in European history, and time never again became ripe for this kind of national rhetoric.

kind of tension which may keep the national project alive and vital. In the Scandinavian countries regionalism has often functioned as a stable and more integrating than threatening element in the national landscape. In some ways the province or region has had the role of providing a micro-level model for patriotism. By learning to love your home region – one part of the national whole – you prepared yourself for national feelings on a higher level, this was the general idea in school education at the beginning of the twentieth century.

At that time in Sweden socialism was often defined as a major threat to national unity, later to be replaced by internationalism or Americanization. We find similar transformations in other nations, depending on the political climate.

This genre of popular debate is perhaps better analysed as a form of cultural contestation, in which different interest groups accuse other groups (or ideologies) of threatening the national ideal. Why do some Swedes at certain times define themselves as more Swedish or better nationalists than others? Why is it that this kind of discourse is more marked in certain historical periods?

It has, for example, sometimes been argued that Swedes are not very chauvinistic, because national slogans or patriotic appeals are less common here than, for example, in the United States or in Romania. But national arguments or national feelings are mainly activated in situations of uncertainty or anxiety. The incessant talk about American morals and values in the United States does not necessarily mean that Americans are more patriotic (or chauvinistic), but rather that the national identity has to be constantly reaffirmed because it is a somewhat fragile construction. The ethnic mix and fluidity calls for a constant remaking of America.

In the Sweden of the 1960s and 70s flag-waving and patriotic rhetoric were definitely *out*, at least in intellectual circles, but this was a period of national stability. In the political turbulence of the 1920s and 30s national rhetoric was a tool of political struggle between the left and the right. The conservatives argued that the social democrats were unpatriotic and out to destroy both traditions and the national heritage. Unlike their counterparts in France and Britain, the Swedish social democrats were, however, very successful in projecting an image of themselves as working "in the best interests of the whole nation". In a way they wrested the national argument from the hands of the conservatives and made it a part of their National Welfare programme. One symbolic manifestation of this change was the introduction of the national flag into the May Day demonstrations during the 1930s.

This was a period when the concept of citizenship

became central in the national rhetoric about the making of a modern nation, populated by modern individuals who had been freed from traditional collective loyalties in order be nationalized as citizens of the new Modern Sweden. The constant references to the many rights and obligations of citizenship – a status which only the nation can give its people – was very typical of this period of nation-building.

Although the social democratic utopia usually called The People's Home was very much part of a project of modernity with eyes directed forward rather than to the past, there was also an attempt to redefine the national heritage. In the 1930s Swedish democracy was still a young institution and in shaping a new national history, great emphasis was placed upon the *democratic* traditions of Sweden (and above all the Swedish peasantry). The ethnologists joined in this redefinition. The traditional villages could now be described as the cradles of democracy, as "the moulds in which the Swedish folk mentality had been shaped, the setting in which our people has gained its basic social instincts" (after Johansson 1987: 7). New combinations of national heroes and villains were also produced.

In the 1930s we can thus analyse how a new national heritage is constructed with new symbols of common ancestry and identity, and the same type of analysis could be carried out for the end of the nineteenth century, when conservatives and liberals fought over the true national values and genuine heritage. (Cf. also Patrick Wright's discussion [1985] of the political struggle over definitions of the national heritage between Labour and Conservatives in postwar England.)

The discourse on national disintegration often misses the fact that national culture is constantly redefined. Every new generation produces its own national sharing and frames of reference, selecting items from the symbolic estate of earlier generations. It is usually not the nation that is falling apart but rather an older version of the national ideal. When indignant protests are made about Swedish schoolchildren who (supposedly) call the national anthem the "ice hockey song" because they only hear it at international matches, people forget that only a few generations of Swedes have ever learnt to sing it.

In 1935 another national event led to a competition for a monument celebrating what was seen as the first meeting of the Swedish parliament in 1435. This time the object was a statue of the peasant rebel leader Engelbrekt from that turbulent period of Swedish history, who was used as a national symbol by both the right and the left. Many social democrats chose to see Engelbrekt as a symbol of early democratic and egalitarian strivings, thereby underlining the political parallels between the 1430s and the 1930s. The sculptor Bror Hjorth's contribution expressed this version of Engelbrekt, who was depicted as a popular leader and forceful agitator, but the official committee found his version too revolutionary and chose a milder and more conventional image of Engelbrekt. (Cf. the discussion in Johannesson 1985.)

This constant redefinition of a national symbolic and cultural capital can be analysed by trying to trace what kind of sharing has united different Swedes (say, a clergyman, a farm woman and an industrial worker) in 1880, in 1930 or today. I would maintain that the sharing is greater today than in the past, but different. Maurice Agulhon has, for example, argued

The caption to this cartoon from 1905 runs:

> *A traitor to his country.*
> *The policeman: What the devil is wrong with you, sir?*
> *– I am sorry, my good constable, but I just couldn't muster the strength to rise when they sang the anthem for the 82nd time.*

The decades around 1900 were a period of intense production (and singing) of patriotic songs in Sweden, and community singing had another peak period during the Second World War (and even more so in occupied Denmark, cf. Karlsson 1988: 155ff.).

Benedict Anderson has pointed out the strong emotional charge in this kind of national ritual: "No matter how banal the words and mediocre the tunes, there is in this singing an experience of simultaneity. At precisely such moments, people wholly unknown to each other utter the same verses to the same melody. The image: unisonance. Singing the Marseillaise, Waltzing Matilda, and Indonesia Raya provides occasions for unisonality, for the echoed psychological realization of the imagined community" (Anderson 1983: 132). A more recent example of this is the key role of patriotic collective singing in the 1988 demonstrations for national revival in the Baltic states.

Many of the national rituals, like hoisting the flag, visiting a national shrine or breaking out in song, appeal more to emotions and gut reactions than to intellectual reasoning. Even the most ardent anti-nationalist may find himself fighting a lump in the throat at such occasions.

that France today is more *culturally* homogenous than during the nineteenth century, but that the *national*, symbolic capital (i.e. the patriotic school book culture) has diminished (Agulhon 1987).

In the same way national rhetoric tends to change. Arguments or language of earlier periods may sound bombastic, chauvinistic or even racist to our modern ears, but we have at the same time developed new forms of rhetoric about the superiority of our own country, which we do not think of as chauvinistic. In his paper on sports and nationalism below, Billy Ehn points out that nationalistic arguments and rhetoric which in other settings or arenas would sound bombastic flourish in the sport pages.

National Culture as Rhetoric and Practice

During the last two centuries nationalism has evolved as a strong source of cultural and social identity, and so far we have little evidence that it is dying, although it may often be dormant. The symbolic community of the nation still produces strong feelings and strong commitments as well as gut reactions of love, hate, pride and aggression. Flag-waving or flag-burning is still, in most settings, no laughing matter.

In this paper, I have argued for a historical anthropology of national cultures, focusing on some of the processes which develop, reproduce and change national identity and culture. This is a field of study which calls not only for a historical but also a comparative approach. Elusive phenomena like Swedishness or Hungarianness are best studied in contrast.

The comparative study of the ways in which nations are turned into cultural formations may benefit from separating three levels. First of all, there exists what we could call an *international cultural grammar* of nationhood, with a thesaurus of general ideas about the cultural ingredients needed to form a nation, like the check-list I mentioned earlier. This includes a symbolic estate (flag, anthem, national landscape, sacred texts, etc.), ideas about a national heritage (a national history and literature, a national folk culture, etc.), as well as notions of national character, values and tastes. This international grammar may also contain specific ideas about the institutional framework. During the nineteenth century it was not only a concept of national folk culture that was circulated between (mainly) European nations, but also guidelines for the proper establishment of institutions like national folk museums and archives, to name one example.

The international thesaurus is transformed into a specific *national lexicon*, local forms of cultural expression, which tend to vary from nation to nation. In this field we can observe how national rhetoric and symbols may be located in different arenas, emphasized in different historical periods or social situations. The third term, *dialect vocabulary*, focuses on the internal divisions within the nation: conflict groups and interests using national arguments and rhetoric, sometimes also creating different styles of national discourse, accusing each other of "vulgar nationalism", "unpatriotic behaviour" or just representing the wrong type of Swedishness. The definition of the Swedish folk heritage of the late nineteenth-century bourgeoisie differed a great deal from that of the social democrats of the 1930s.

Whereas the concept of nationalism is relatively clearly defined as a political ideology, national culture is a term which often contains a mixture of normative and descriptive elements. I have argued for a focus on the everyday level of cultural sharing, which happens to be contained by national borders: the shared understandings and frames of references of Swedes or Hungarians.

In the study of the ways in which culture is *nationalized* we thus have to distinguish between two processes. One is concerned with the ways in which cultural elements are turned into symbols or national rhetoric – declared to symbolize the essence of the nation or its inhabitants or stated as norms about proper national behaviour and virtues; the other has to do with how cultural flows are contained, organized and transformed within the national borders – how national space becomes cultural space. This also calls for an analysis of the ways in which different cultural domains are nationalized, from landscape to sport, or perhaps even denationalized at later stages, as in the case with national symbols which lose their power or meaning.

In looking at national culture as process it is important to avoid a narrative structure based upon an evolutionary or devolutionary perspective, in which nations are born, come of age or fade away, to name a few common life cycle metaphors in studies of nationalism. Modern nationalism is a cultural paradigm, but all nations do not go through identical processes of making and remaking. Take the question of timing: when are certain national strategies, claims or rhetorics legitimate and successful or just futile or even comical?[7] The erection of a national monument in Budapest in 1896 created a national rallying point, whereas in Sweden in 1909 the same plans proved to be a total flop.

Nationalism may often be a dormant cultural force, activated only situationally and selectively. National identity is not always an overriding loyalty and there are social groups which may combine a very international and cosmopolitan identity with a sense of national belonging.

In 1882 the Frenchman Joseph Ernest Roman gave his classic definition of a nation having to be something more than a mere customs union, a true nation must have a soul, he added in the style of contemporary speech and continued:

> L'existence d'une nation est (pardonnez moi cette métaphore) un plébiscite de tous les jours, comme l'existence de l'individu est une affirmation perpétuelle de vie. (Quoted after Østergaard 1988: 29)

It is this problem of how the nation is reaffirmed by its national subjects in "daily referendums" that perhaps is the least developed theme in studies of national culture-building. The national project cannot survive as a mere ideological construction, it must exist as a cultural praxis in everyday life. Being Swedish is a kind of experience which is activated in watching the Olympics on TV, in hoisting the flag for a family reunion, in making ironic comments about the Swedish national character (and feeling hurt when non-Swedes make similar remarks), in memories of holiday trips to national sights, or in feelings of being out of place on the wrong side of the national border and securely at home on the inside, in the sharing of national frames of references, from jokes to images.

We need to devote a lot more attention to how this kind of national sharing is produced and reproduced in everyday life, asking how deep, how long and how wide it is at given times and in different social settings, and how it varies from generation to generation. A study of this process, thus, calls for an analysis, not so much of rhetoric but of practice, of the lived national experience.

Notes

1 A version of this paper was presented at the 12th International Congress of Anthropological and Ethnological Sciences in Zagreb, 24–31 July, 1988, in the session on History and Anthropology, and I am grateful for the stimulating comments put forward at this session. Special thanks also to Alan Crozier for his help with the translation and his constructive remarks.

2 The first workshop on "National Culture as Process" in Budapest, 1–3 May 1989, also included papers by Tamás Hofer and two Hungarian sociologists, György Csepeli and Judit Lendvay, as well as contributions by the Swedish historian Bo Öhngren and the ethnologist Anders Lundin.

3 The interest in cultural perspectives on nation-building among historians is expressed in works like Weber (1976), Hobsbawm & Ranger (1983), Braudel (1986) and Agulhon (1987) (see also the excellent overview in Østergaard 1988), whereas recent examples of anthropologists dealing with the cultural politics of nationalism are found in studies by, for example, Herzfeld (1987) and Kapferer (1988).

4 See the discussion on the nationalization of Dalecarlia in Rosander (1986) and the similar Norwegian processes in Berggreen (1989) and the general discussion in Oinas (1978).

5 The metaphor of a North-South dichotomy in national stereotypes was developed by Tomas Gerholm in a colloquium on national mentalities at Lund University in 1985.

6 The changing Hungarian cultural construction of national identity and the stereotyping of other nations were discussed at the seminar in two contributions by György Csepeli (n.d.) and Judit Lendvay (n.d.). For a discussion of the changing stereotypes of Danes and Swedes over the last century, see the discussion in Löfgren (1986) and Linde-Laursen (n.d.). A general discussion of national stereotypes is found in the Dutch anthropological journal *Foocal: Tijdschrift voor Anthropologie*, April 1986, which presents material from a colloquy on national character.

7 See the discussion of the timing of the claim to nationhood in Smith (1986: 8ff.) and Gellner (1983).

References

Agulhon, Maurice 1981: *Marianne into Battle: Republican Image and Symbolism in France 1789–1880*. Cambridge: Cambridge Univ. Press.

Agulhon, Maurice 1987: La fabrication de la France: Problèmes et controverses. *Anthropologie Sociale et Ethnologie de la France: Colloque du Centre d'éthnologie française et du Musée national des arts et traditions populaires*. Paris: Mimeograph.

Anderson, Benedict 1983: *Imagined Communities: Reflections on the Origin and Spread of Nationalism*. London: Verso.

Benedict, Burton 1983: *The Anthropology of World's Fairs: San Francisco's Panama Pacific International Exposition of 1915*. London: Scholar Press.

Berggreen, Brit 1989: *Da kulturen kom till Norge*. Oslo: Aschehoug.

Biörnstad, Arne 1976: Svenska flaggans bruk. *Fataburen* 1976, 43–56.

Braudel, Fernand 1986: *L'Identité de la France*, I–III. Paris: Arthaud-Flammarion.

Colls, Robert & Philip Dodd (eds.) 1986: *Englishness: Politics and Culture 1880–1920*. Beckenham: Croom Helm.

Crump, Jeremy 1986: The Identity of English Music: The Reception of Elgar 1898–1935. In: Colls & Dodd, op.cit., 164–190.

Csepeli, György (n.d.): The Social Construction of National Identity in Contemporary Hungary. Paper presented at the seminar "National culture as process: Hungarian and Swedish experiences", Budapest May 1–3, 1989.

Daun, Åke & Billy Ehn 1988: *Blandsverige*. Stockholm: Carlsson.

Ehn, Billy 1983: *Ska vi leka tiger? Daghemsliv ur kulturell synvinkel*. Malmö: Liber.

Elias, Norbert (1939)1978: *The Civilizing Process: The History of Manners*. Oxford: Blackwell.

Eliot, T.S. 1949: *Notes towards the Definition of Culture*. New York: Harcourt.

Firth, Raymond 1973: *Symbols: Public and Private*. London.

Frykman, Jonas & Orvar Löfgren 1987: *Culture Builders: A Historical Anthropology of Middle-Class Life*. New Brunswick: Rutgers Univ. Press.

Furuland, Lars 1987: "Lyssna till den granens susning": Om en läsebok som folkuppfostrare. *Kungl. Vitterhets Historie och Antikvitets Akademiens Årsbok* 1987, 1–15.

Gellner, Ernest 1983: *Nations and Nationalism*. Oxford: Blackwell.

Hannerz, Ulf n.d.: American Culture: Creolized, Creolizing. Paper presented at the Nordic Association for American Studies, Uppsala.

Harbsmeier, Michael 1986: Danmark: Nation, kultur og køn. *Stofskifte* 13, 47–74.

Herzfeld, Michael 1982: *Ours Once More: Folklore, Ideology, and the Making of the Modern Greece*. Austin: Univ. of Texas Press.
Herzfeld, Michael 1987: *Anthropology through the Looking Glass: Critical Ethnography in the Margins of Europe*. Cambridge: Cambridge University Press.
Hobsbawm, Eric & Terence Ranger (eds.) 1983: *The Invention of Tradition*. London.
Hofer, Tamás n.d.: Constructing the Heritage of Hungarian Folk Culture: Symbolic Uses of Peasant Traditions. Paper presented at the seminar "National culture as process: Hungarian and Swedish experiences".
Honko, Lauri (ed.) 1980: *Folklore och nationsbyggande i Norden*. Åbo: NIF.
Johannesson, Kurt 1985: Engelbrekt och upprorens retorik. *Artes* 2, 87–102.
Johansson, Ella 1987: Vår stolta särprägel: Nationalism i svensk etnologi. *Nord-Nytt* 30.
Kapferer, Bruce 1988: *Legends of People: Myths of State. Violence, Intolerance and Political Culture in Sri Lanka and Australia*. Washington: Smithsonian Institution Press.
Karlsson, Henrik 1988: *O, ädle svensk! Biskop Thomas' frihetssång i musik och politik*. (Kungl. Musikaliska akademiens skriftserie, 59.)
Lendvay, Judit n.d.: National Auto- and Hetero-Stereotypes Concerning Hungary and Hungarians. Paper presented at the seminar "National culture as process: Hungarian and Swedish experiences", Budapest May 1–3, 1989.
Linde-Laursen, Anders n.d.: *Fra u-land til storebror: Danskernes syn på svenskere og Sverige i det tyvende århundrede*. (Unpublished ms.)
Löfgren, Orvar 1985: Kring nationalkänslans kulturella organisation. *Nord-Nytt* 25, 73–85.
Löfgren, Orvar 1986: Deconstructing Swedishness: Class and Culture in Modern Sweden. In: *Anthropology at Home*, ed. Anthony Jackson. ASA Monographs 25. London: Tavistock.
Löfgren, Orvar 1987: Om behovet for danskhed. *Hug* 47, 49–55.
Löfgren, Orvar 1987: Colonizing the Territory of Historical Anthropology. *Culture & History* 1, 7–30.
Löfgren, Orvar 1989: Landscapes and Mindscapes. *Folk* 31, 183–208.
Löfgren, Orvar n.d.: Medierna i nationsbygget. Forthcoming in *Medier och kulturell förändring*, ed. Ulf Hannerz.
Marchand, Roland 1985: *Advertising the American Dream: Making Way for Modernity 1920–1940*. Berkeley: Univ. of California Press.
Nordstedt, J.F. 1985: *I Sverige*. Stockholm.
Oinas, Felix J. (ed.) 1978: *Folklore, Nationalism and Politics*. Columbus: Slavica.
Østergaard, Uffe 1988: *Hvad er en nationsstat?* Arbejdspapir nr. 12, Center for Kulturforskning, Århus University.
Østerud, Øyvind 1986: Nationalstaten Norge en karakteriserende skisse. In: *Det norske samfunn*, ed. Lars Alldén et al., 9–32. Oslo: Gyldendal.
Rosander, Göran 1986: The "Nationalization" of Dalecarlia. How a Special Province Became a National Symbol for Sweden. *Arv* 42, 93–142.
Rosander, Göran (ed.) 1987: *Turisternas Leksand*. (Leksand sockenbeskrivning, IX.)
Rydell, Robert W. 1984: *All the World's a Fair: Visions of Empire at American International Expositions, 1876–1916*. Chicago: Univ. of Chicago Press.
Schlesinger, Philip 1987: On National Identity: Some Conceptions and Misconceptions Criticized. *Social Science Information* 26:2, 219–264.
Smeds, Kerstin 1983: Finland på världsutställningen i Paris 1889. *Historisk tidskrift för Finland* 2, 81–102.
Smith, Anthony D. 1986: *The Ethnic Origins of Nations*. Oxford: Blackwell.
Teleman, Ulf (ed.) 1986: *De nordiske skriftspråkenes utvikling på 1800-tallet*, 3. *Ideologier og språkstyring*. Oslo: Nordisk språksekretariats rapporter 7.
Whisnant, David E. 1983: *All that is Native and Fine: The Politics of Culture in an American Region*. Chapel Hill: Univ. of North Carolina Press.
Williams, Raymond 1977: *Marxism and Literature*. Oxford: Oxford Univ. Press.
Wright, Patrick 1985: *On Living in an Old Country: The National Past in Contemporary Britain*. London: Verso.

Orvar Löfgren, Professor emeritus in European Ethnology at the Department of Cultural Sciences, Lund University, Sweden. The cultural analysis and ethnography of everyday life has been an ongoing focus in his research. Central research fields have been studies of national identity and transnational mobility, media and consumption.
(orvar.lofgren@kultur.lu.se)

THE PLACE OF CULTURE(S) REVISITED
Reading Konrad Köstlin

Nevena Škrbić Alempijević, University of Zagreb

What marked European ethnology in Croatia during the 1990s, in which my generation of ethnologists graduated, was a certain disciplinary identity crisis and a prevalent feeling of frustration. Many of us felt as if we were somehow caught in between theory and practice. Such a situation was in line with global tendencies within humanities and social sciences and can partly be understood as an echo of poststructuralist critique of classificatory systems, singular meanings and absolute truths. It was a time when the linguistic turn was strongly felt in the humanities and the seemingly solid grounds of ethnological and folklorist knowledge-making and mapping of cultures were thoroughly debunked through critical analyses of the discursive construction of social phenomena and processes. On the other hand, the specific political and social context in Croatia in the early 1990s, the break-up of Yugoslavia and the wars that ensued, the declaration of Croatia's independence and the country's transition from socialism, undoubtedly left a strong mark on research interests and approaches among Croatian ethnologists and folklorists in that period. Images of the Croatian state, culture and traditions were constructed anew, as an indisputable value. Ethnologists were expected, and invited, to contribute to the discovery and reinterpretation of the Croatian heritage, which made them balance between the imperative to preserve, present and construct heritage on the one hand and their aptitude to critically observe the phenomena on the other. Analyses of ethnic and national identification processes, studies of safeguarding and preservation of war-threatened cultural heritage, war ethnography, texts on forced migrations and Croatian diaspora proliferated at that time.

In academic circles, there was an intensive debate about the hierarchy of disciplinary knowledge production, about the limitations of the focus on folk culture as an object of study and, of the way it had been approached in the study programme we had just finished. At the same time, museums, conservation and restoration departments and other heritage institutions were amongst the most common employers of ethnologists. Policymakers expected us to deliver our expertise on culture no matter how constructed it was. What I myself encountered in my work as a museum curator were concrete objects waiting for me to document, classify, preserve, analyse, problematise and contextualise and finally to be put on display. Among people who visited cultural institutions these museological objects mattered for various reasons. They were ready to share their narrations about those objects with me, willing to see them as segments of a museum exhibition, or eager to record the material as a shot in a cultural-tourism promotional video with the intention of displaying the beauty and diversity of the region and the country.

Ethnologia Europaea pointed to the dilemmas and potentials of ethnological research at the turn of the twenty-first century with articles that discussed the materiality that people experience through their bodies and all their senses, ways of being in the lived world, practices of everyday life, space and the crea-

Nevena Škrbić Alempijević 2017: The Place of Culture(s) Revisited: Reading Konrad Köstlin.
Ethnologia Europaea 47:1, 54–57. © Museum Tusculanum Press.

tion of its borders, the contemporary life of traditional culture and so on. Those contributions clearly indicated that in-depth ethnological studies of the dynamics of culture, observed simultaneously as a social construct and reality, as Konrad Köstlin (1981) once formulated it, are greatly needed in a changing world. And that is where Köstlin's article on "Vanishing Borders and the Rise of Culture(s)" (*Ethnologia Europaea* vol. 29:2, 1999) comes into play for me. Although having fully acquired the conceptual and methodological shifts in relation to poststructuralism and deconstructivism, the author shows that we cannot pronounce "the death of the subject" of ethnological and folklorist inquiry. He insists that we cannot turn a blind eye to the contemporary "stress on culture", that is, to the omnipresent tendency of evoking, using and (re)constructing culture, including components of folk culture, by different agents and for various purposes.

His text begins with a prologue that draws the reader's attention to traits of folk culture that have been treated in earlier ethnographic texts as monuments of "the rural way of life", but which also function as landmarks in our discipline's past due to their long-term central status in ethnological and folklorist research. He vividly describes elements of rural architecture in Lower Austria, in particular the phenomenon of *Kellergassen* (lanes with wine cellars), as well as the practices, divisions, perceptions and worldviews connected to them. However, Köstlin approaches these spaces and social lives from a different angle in comparison with his ethnological predecessors. His refreshing view of the everyday life of wine-producers focuses on the present "power of what is called culture" (p. 36): on the production of difference as identity by means of folk culture and on the creation of distinctive local, regional, and European cultural spaces. Previous ethnological classifications and mappings of folk culture had contributed significantly to that political project, he notes, by spotting distinctive features and delineating boundaries between different culture zones.

What Köstlin lays out before us in his text are the mechanisms by which a symbolic geography is imagined and implemented in a world where political borders had been opened and the walls and wires removed – at least temporarily and at least in the part of Europe from which he writes. At the same instance, some new boundaries, not less concrete, are activated on the basis of pools of cultural differences, imagological representations of regions and stereotypes about "us" and "them". People seem to need and like borders, Köstlin concludes, because such schemes and limitations provide them with a sense of continuity and certainty in a world where political frontiers have allegedly vanished and long-established orders have been contested (p. 33). Borders, albeit cultural ones, are also the imperative of politics, which needs a territory to govern. In this way, narratives about cultural "unity and diversity", integrated in the foundations of folklore studies, also represent formative myths for the creation of regions.

For Köstlin, regions emerge at the intersection of human intersubjectivities, cultural and spatial potentialities and actualities. Fashioning cultural areas is explained as one of the main current trends in the making of places: places where we are and places where we want to be. In order to define cultural difference as identity and anchor it to space, regional borders have been revitalised, but also broadened and made more flexible. For many people, their position within a region functions as a claim of their rightful participation in the new order of things and as a strategy of joining a "Europe of regions" (p. 31). Regional identification dimension has thus become one of the ways in which people argue for their belonging to Europe. Criteria for the construction of regional difference largely rely on what they want to break away from, which layers of their pasts they want to forget. This was especially the case in Croatia in the period preceding the country's accession to the European Union in 2013. Belonging to Central Europe (*Mitteleuropa*) and the Mediterranean – the regions used by Köstlin as showcases of the way in which the borders of cultural areas are (re)defined – has been declared by cultural policymakers as a desirable identity strategy in Croatia, as well as an undisputable fact. The analysis of cultural-touristic, academic, political and popular discourses, but also of everyday practices, provides us with an understanding of why it is important for people to be Central European (mostly in the case of the continental part of Croatia) or Mediterranean (among people living in Croatia's coastal part). These regions have gained prominence as markers of Croatian political and economic dispositions housed within the framework of the EU. However, the assigning of Croatia to these cultural regions is not only the claim where its inhabitants see themselves in the future, a mechanism of the country's Europeanization. It is also Croatians' attempt to distance themselves from others – primarily from the association with the former Yugoslavia and the imagined Balkans (cf. Todorova 2009).

The inclination to swear new allegiances, establish cultural regions, and turn them into tangible realities was visible in all spheres of Croatian society. In that context, to me as an ethnologist, Köstlin's article served as a clear call for action, urging me to analyse processes that were affecting my life and my self-perception, as well as lives and perceptions of others around me. I actually contributed to these processes as a professional often asked by media to explain the presence of cultural traits that were considered proof of our country's age-old belonging to pro-European regions. So Köstlin's urging to observe "regions while they are under construction", to "read their instruction manuals", to "discuss their selection of mostly historical artefacts as signifiers and see the results" (p. 32) resonated strongly with my work, especially in studies oriented towards the production of Mediterranean heritage and its usage in nation-building processes in Croatia. The approach he proposes deals with Europe both as a cultural construction and a reality felt under one's feet. "Europe as a Cultural Construction and Reality" is actually the title of *Ethnologia Europaea*'s special issue published in 1999 and reprinted in 2001. The contributions comprised in this issue, including Köstlin's article, served as a response to the fast-changing political, economic and social circumstances, which bring forth new symbolic geographies, but also as a recognition that European ethnology should play one of the central roles in researching and generating insights in those processes.

Although published some seventeen years ago, the topics, research questions and approaches to region-making processes as proposed in Köstlin's text still represent a source of inspiration for researchers who tackle the issues of regional identity, place-making, and spatiality. For instance, in 2014 an anthology entitled *Drawing the Boundaries Again: Transformations of Identities and Redefinitions of Cultural Regions in New Political Circumstances* was published as a joint venture between the Croatian and Slovene Ethnological Societies. The topics discussed in the book – the redefining of borders and shifts of mental geographies in the context of ascension to the EU, the materialisation and musealisation of markers of a new identity, the role of ethnology in the locality/region/nation-building processes – indicate that Köstlin's discussions on replacing or strengthening state borders with cultural boundaries are still current today.

Köstlin also argues that not only regions, but also smaller localities, concrete places and homes are spaces that grow in importance in the course of the blurring of national borders. That is to say: the significance of locations is not diminished under the influence of globalisation processes. On the contrary, a renewed interest in local "roots", cultures, and specific features is considered to be a direct outcome of taking a share in worldwide activities. People make a conscious effort, the author states, "to ground their existence locally, despite the fact that they live, act and consume globally" (p. 34). Another related pair that Köstlin views through a similar prism is mobility and the local. These categories are seen as two sides of the same coin, each offering an insight into complex and fluid existences of contemporary citizens of the world, where taking part in both local and transnational communities is not seen as a contradiction. A declared risk of unification, the author believes, actually unleashes the processes of pluralization and searching for distinction. The diversity Köstlin talks about in this context is understood as a source of European strength and richness.

But at what point does the cultural or regional differences become too different? When does it, instead of representing a well of diversity, multiculturalism, and cosmopolitanism, start to be perceived as a threat to the European way of life, values, economy? Does the difference need to have a European origin, or at least a European-like air attributed to it, in order to be tolerated and accepted? In which cases does the appearance of migrating Others who are conceived of as different in respect to their cultures, religions, political attitudes, and lifestyles provoke the "defence" of borders? The political and social circumstances have changed significantly from the time when Konrad Köstlin pointed to the vanishing of borders in Europe. Recently, as a response to the so-called migrant crisis, Europeans have witnessed the reintroduction of national frontiers, the building of new walls, the keeping out of trespassers by barbed wire. However, this re-establishing of old political lines and the search for old certainties does not bring into question Köstlin's main arguments. Indeed, they only shed a new light on the relationship between the significance of political borders and the rise of culture or cultures deemed appropriate within them.

Nevena Škrbić Alempijević is an associate professor at the Department of Ethnology and Cultural Anthropology, Faculty of Humanities and Social Sciences, University of Zagreb, Croatia. Her main research fields are anthropology of social memory, place and space, island studies, performance studies, studies of carnivals, festivals and other public events. Together with Sanja Potkonjak and Tihana Rubić, she has recently prepared the book *Misliti etnografski: Kvalitativni pristupi i metode u etnologiji i kulturnoj antropologiji* [Thinking Ethnographically: Qualitative Strategies and Methods in Ethnology and Cultural Anthropology] (2016).
(nskrbic@ffzg.hr)

VANISHING BORDERS AND THE RISE OF CULTURE(S)

Reprinted from *Ethnologia Europaea* 29:2, 1999

Konrad Köstlin

The article analyses some emerging new functions of "local cultures" and new meanings of so-called "national cultures" in contemporary public discourses. In recent years, we have witnessed the disappearance of old certainties, as the previously-fixed boundaries defining nations and states have become more ambiguous; meanwhile, new cultural frontiers have been erected around other territorial spaces. The argument advanced in this paper mainly in relation to spatiality and local cultures could be extended to values, morals, religion, etc. This is not the return of romantic nineteenth-century ideas; rather, it is suggested here that this phenomenon draws upon the work of folklorists and ethnologists, whose descriptions and mapping of folk cultures is taken as scientific evidence of distinctive local and regional differences.

Keywords: regionalisation, folk culture, regional differences, local cultures, cultural borders, globalisation

Prologue

One of the areas in the province of Lower Austria near the city of Vienna is called *Weinviertel*. Cellars dug in the ground and ranged in rows side by side form the so-called *Kellergassen*, which are narrow passages with cellars on both sides with a little building at the entrance. These small subterranean rooms containing wine presses were built without chimneys; this led to the widespread folk belief that the *Kellergassen* were constructed as decoy villages intended to deceive enemies, especially the Turks. Since the production of wine was understood as a task performed only by men, the *Kellergassen* were described as male places, and this gave rise to numerous stories being written about them. The *Kellergassen* are only a few decades older than *Volkskunde* itself, but the cellars are the subject of a set of narratives created by amateur folklorists. These stories have been invented mainly during the last two centuries which created not only folkloristics but also made the region, located near the city of Vienna, become well-known as holiday resort (Koppensteiner 1997).

The regional government of Lower Austria and its tourist authorities have established the *Kellergassen* as an identity-forming icon of the region – regardless the fact that exactly the same arrangement exists on the other side of the border in Moravia and in Slovakia, not to mention Hungary and some other Austri-

Konrad Köstlin 2017: Vanishing Borders and the Rise of Culture(s). Reprinted from 1999 *Ethnologia Europaea* 29:2, 31–36.
Ethnologia Europaea 47:1, 58–64.

an regions. It may be just by accident that this icon was invented after the opening of the Iron Curtain.

On the Moravian side of the border there is a famous vegetable-gardening area where little cucumbers, *Znaimer Gurkerln*, have been produced since the nineteenth century and were famous all over the monarchy and in Germany. Recently, also after the fall of the Iron Curtain, the farming authorities of the region on the Austrian side of the border near the town of Retz have created a kind of counter-cucumber: the *Retzer Gurkerln*.

When Austria held the EU-presidentship, during the first meeting in the summer of 1998, the Austrian secretary of state Wolfgang Schüssel ceremoniously presented his European colleagues with sports shoes in Austria's red-white-red colours "to make Europe fit". At the second meeting, he gave his colleagues folksy coarse woollen coats from Austria. One could interpret his action as a symbolic attempt to promote the cultural unification of Europe, by inviting everyone to wear Austrian shoes; precisely the opposite was intended: a promotion of differences following the theory of a Europe of regions which is offered by EU publicists to counter the fear of a "European stew". Austria nonetheless performed its presidentship by means of its nationalized culture, festivities, waltzes, folk culture and *Mozartkugeln* – as the EU's clichés demanded.

In 1998 it was reported that children in a communal kindergarten in Berlin had painted cows the way they knew from ads: violet and white-speckled. The kids had taken their image of reality from the Milka cow in TV commercials. When Switzerland celebrated its national holiday this year on August 1st, the city of Zürich was filled with hundreds of plastic cows. The cowization of Switzerland seems to be a part of a strategy to apply to the most perfectly industrialized country an image of the most perfectly domesticated rurality. Quotations are taken from the national mythology of the Swiss herdsmen, rather than from the precision toolmaker. The result is a very effectively imaged reality which seems to be easy to handle.

Lately the revision of the Silk Road was brought up, re-enacting the historical commercial trade between Europe and China, thus supporting and smoothing new commerce and market orientations. The architecture of the Habsburgian Monarchy – especially the resemblance between the opera houses from Vienna, Trieste, Pécs, Karlsbad or Brno – which were built by the same architects, were used as evidence to (re-?)construct a new idea of a central Europe ("Mitteleuropa") which is now to be located much more east than ever before (Magris 1993). An *Institut für den Donauraum* develops and puts forward an idealistic vision of the multiethnic Austrian Empire as a basis for new cultural alliances, and shapes a vision of a specific Austrian responsibility for the area. The glorification of the K.u.K.-Monarchy is now to be followed by the clarification of the lapsed Osmanian Empire in which the mechanics of tolerance towards the non-Turkish population in the Balkan area is to be focused upon in a series of Balkan studies (*Ethnologia Balkanica* 1997ff.; *Ethnographia Bulgarica* 1978). All this happens by using markers which are declared to be cultural ones. "Jede Generation wählt sich Trümmer aus der Vergangenheit und fügt sie entsprechend den eigenen Idealen und Wertungen zu Häusern eigener Art zusammen" (Elias 1969).

The Story of the Fallen Borders

"Die alten Grenzen sind gefallen" was the title of an article concerning Salzburg's *Galerie Fotohof*, which deals in modern photography in Austria, praising the gallery as the country's top address for contemporary photography. The title of the exhibition was *Offene Grenzen* (Sonna 1998). The idea of falling walls and opening borders has become so popular in every context that it seems to be heard and read everywhere. Media writers and people talk of the "borders" of sexuality, of shame, of classes, of states, etc., which now seem to be vanishing or more or less unimportant. The publication of the Clinton-Lewinsky videos, on the other hand, seems to underline the seemingly absolute lack of limitations; the public reaction provoked a demand for moral guidelines and boundaries of good taste.

The story finds its counter story: while state borders are seeming to become less important, the selling-out of national enterprises to multinational buyers is perceived not only as a loss of familiar, everyday array but also and apparently more importantly as a national cultural tragedy. Social borders of classes and class differences which seemed to be very strict are being replaced by the more or less vague milieus or taste zones, which are not defined as sharply and seem to be very fluid, flowing across former social boundaries. On the other hand we can observe how new regions are being fashioned everywhere, we can watch them while they are under construction, we can read their instruction manuals, discuss their selection of mostly historical artefacts as signifiers and see the results. In Austria, a great number of new regions have been established the last decade, not only for touristic purposes (Senker 1998).

Fashioning Cultural Areas

Not surprisingly, then (but perhaps a bit ironically), the title of a conference in Zagreb in October 1998 was "Where Does the Mediterranean begin?". "Mediterranean" might refer to the commonplace notion of a broadly similar set of cultural patterns which unites the area around the Mediterranean sea, which the Italian fascism defined strictly in national terms, calling it "mare nostro". It also refers to the idea of a longue durée of economic and ecological claims upon, and about it, by the nations which share its shores; and, subsequently, there developed cultural similarities around the Mediterranean, an idea which was developed by Fernand Braudel and the Annales group. But Braudel's argument for an ecologically-based mentality has an inclination towards continuity and can be used as an anti-Balkanic version of a newly-created and thus historically-rooted identity which orientates some countries towards Europe and others away from it. European in this regard is perceived as opposite to the Balkanian (Rihtman-Auguštin 1998). It may work quite well and it may separate the good ones from the bad ones, changing the paradigm and using Balkanic and anti-Balkanic patterns. Today we can observe that the commonalities of a region are no longer only a matter of self-evident history but are, above all, definitions created by an elite of word- and idea-coiners using any kind of histories quite arbitrarily. History can be one of the pieces of evidence quoted to create a region. The German politician Björn Engholm (a well-known aficionado of the Toscana lifestyle) propounded the idea of the Baltic Sea as the "Mittelmeer des Nordens" and initiated the "Ars Baltica" in 1987.

Simply by renaming Samuel Huntington's *The Clash of Civilizations* (Huntington 1997) as "the clash of cultures" changes its function and contours. Most people use the phrase and discuss the idea without having read the book. The title fits well into contemporary discourses and produces its own reality, often far from the author's intentions. Cultural borders seem to have replaced state borders. But *Offene Grenzen* can also mean that a kind of undisciplined freedom (*Narrenfreiheit*) has taken centre-stage. On the other hand – as mentioned above – people seem to need borders, limitations and visible, touchable, reliable schemes of orderliness and predictability. Since the old orders are breaking down, we need to invent new ones to replace them (Foucault 1970); to tame and civilise formless chaos by naming and classifying its constituents – imposing our cultural scheme upon them. This is one of the leading ideas of modernity that we do not seem to be able to discard. Post-modernity merely changes the labels. Nowadays, we talk more than ever about eras, epochs, we predict "decisive historical moments", we think about breaks with the past, and liminal passages from one thing to another, quoting Victor Turner or Arnold van Gennep over and over again (Turner 1981) – all this, ironically, is a reflection on order and regularity rather than their absence.

The Stress on Culture

Culture in this context can be everything. In France, soccer has become so important that Pierre Bourdieu and Marc Augé comment on it and describe it as a new form of national communion which has become transformed from the virtual reality of television images to the currency of Frenchness in the streets of the nation. The virtuality of peaceful multi-ethnic nation, united in *le fotball*, obscured another reality, at least for a time. Jacques Chirac and Lionel Jospin, thanks to the national soccer team, were more popular than ever before. The less they actually did, the higher their popularity index was. *La cohabitation* between socialists and conservatives also worked better than ever. Both President and Prime Minister took their vacations at the same time, a thing that had never happened before (Altwegg 1998). *La Marseillaise* was sung more frequently, and analysts had claimed a new multicultural euphoria had overtaken the nation – so that Jean Le Pen's radicals seem to be out of the game. The right wing, with its national biological primordialism, was overwhelmed then by the new liberal religion of sport which formed the nation anew by means of culture. Quite similarly Croatia's national pride was enormously increased by the fact that their national team had beaten the German football team and the accent on sport as culture made the country, including its government, obviously more acceptable within Europe.

Today anything can be marked as "culture", as we know, "high" culture in the sense of the beaux-arts as in the Austrian case, where the Chancellor of the republic himself is in charge of culture and is called *Kulturkanzler*. Culture functions as a national enterprise and a mark of distinction just because someone says so – and if others believe it because of a certain and mostly historical plausibility, it can work out quite well.

Since the "old" borders have vanished, new ones have had to be erected. These are not always smaller regions for touristic purposes, of the kind mentioned above. Local "roots" and culture, rather than class, are becoming the currency of contemporary identity discourses. The region and its cultural infrastructure dominates as the identity-marker. The German philosopher Eduard Spranger wrote about roots in a small but influential book first published in 1923, warning: *Weh' dem, der nirgends wurzelt* (Spranger 1953). Hermann Lübbe, a German social philosopher, has described modern regionalism as a compensation for the ongoing vagueness in modernity of social rootedness (Lübbe 1981). If it is true that people are no longer socially incorporated into communities in the ways that they used to be, and if it is true that people – as Foucault said – have fallen out of a given social order, then contemporary authenticities are created by individuals doing their own identity-working (Bendix 1997). The more globalists praise their worldwide activities, the more people localize themselves in doing so. Even in the globalisation argument, the promotion of differences mingles with the metaphor of the soil, the regional. People more and more try to ground their existence locally, despite the fact that they live, act and consume globally (Köstlin 2000).

Musealising the Local

The process of musealisation (Zacharias 1990) of the local shows to what degree we have learned to declare and to decipher our existence by means of stories concerning the region or the localities in which we live. Today the difference between North Germany and the South, for instance, is obscured only by the rhetorics of the division between East and West. Yet it could be argued that the German East of the former DDR from a Southern perspective has very clear connotations of the old and heartily-disliked North: Protestant, less comfortable, less authentically German.

Regions are fashioned today by means of culture: in Austria, a series of CDs is called *Musik der Regionen* thus describing and defining regions which never before existed in such homogeneous cultural terms. Folklore experts today judge certain types of music as "wrong" or "right" for any given area. Folk costumes and folk songs have acquired new standardised and stereotyped meanings and moral value as identity-markers. The mapping of folk-culture elements in ethnographic atlases established regions and the cultural borders between them anew. Typicalities and statistical frequencies, in other people's hands, readily become transformed into icons and stereotypes. Thus, a speaker on a carnival presentation on TV could comment that a certain type of costume (*Weißnarren in der Baar*) did fit in the region: an after-effect of ethnographic mapping in the fifties. Again: a new demand for the delineation of borders has arisen as a consequence of our having said that the old ones have vanished.

Mobility and the Local

To be prepared for mobility has become one of the central values within the ideology of globalisation, which some criticise as a fetish. But by the same process people (and sometimes the very same people) root themselves in their locality. They root themselves symbolically by eating local food, wearing local accessories or costumes and consuming and celebrating local customs. In Tyrol dumplings are used as identity markers and thus become – as Tyrolean dumplings – regional soul-food (Köstlin 1977) – even if some people don't really like to eat them.

Unity and diversity: we handle both; we observe our world becoming more and more unified on the one hand, and on the other more and more disjointed. Unification seems to provoke a process of pluralisation and multiplexity. As the global nets small entities, regions gain more and more importance. Those two parallel and synchronous tendencies of unification and multiplexity, of mobility and the search for locality are contradictory only on the surface. They are a single phenomenon within the process of modernisation. The McDonaldisation of the world and its regionalisation by means of culture are result of the internationalisation of particular forms of modernity which became established long before the word "globalization" was coined and the process was brought so sharply into view. The rise of regional food and nationalism that is so visible today belong to that phenomenon, which we now call globalisation (Köstlin 1996).

Difference as Identity

What we call folk culture has been described and in manifold ways offered as one of the main resources for what is called identity by means of distinction and differentiation. Its paradox is that people's social roles have become transformed. Modern states, and those states which preceded them, which strove to forge their own identities as nations by unifying, universalising, centralising, and standardising have redefined the individual's primary role relationships as being those of a citizen of the state, subject to its laws, rather than to those relationships arising from kinship, community, and custom. From this has emerged a new diversity of *Stämme*, of regionalistic movements and tribes of Hyphen-Americans (Byron 1995) playing mostly harmless symbolic games which well-entrenched modern states can afford to tolerate or even to indulge (Köstlin 1979). Today, emphasising their local rootedness has become more important for a segment of our society than profession – and even managers use their roots as a resource to manipulate workers and customers to their companies' advantage.

Since the importance of leisure-time has increased in people's lives, and – according to its interpreters – is expected to be experienced as creative and self-actualising, it has become the field of modern man's identity-puzzle. More frequently people now have to perceive their identities as non-employed ones. Folk culture offers itself as a something which helps to articulate and produce diversities, which can be incorporated into modern life-styles. Even people like Arjun Appadurai mention that they live in more than one locality, and using the argument of the anti-local, they celebrate their existence as culturally patterned by diverse worlds of localities.

Given this background, folk culture and regionalism make new sense. They diminish and avoid or euphemize the negative connotations of mass culture. Its localised and culturally-defined borders provide the means to accentuate uniqueness and stake claims to distinction. Regional and local culture stand for distinctiveness. In our traditional disciplinary discourses, we have promoted the differences and have neglected the similarities. Folk cultures have been treated as distinct, a priori. The distinctiveness of regional and local specialities is taken for granted. They are described and perceived as "genuine", "authentic" and "historically-rooted". Folk culture, put in the scene like other types of quotations, mingles among the stage props in the theatre of modernity: folk culture in this perspective is clearly avant-garde. It is the most modern culture, promising to offer the central markers of identity. Its programme contains multi-vocality, distinction, uniqueness and authenticity plus democracy; and everybody seems to be empowered to take part in the game. On the other hand it seems to be something which can effectively oppose and counter the homogenising processes of modernity. Yet folk culture's attractiveness is to be understood only beyond the horizon of modernization, regardless the fact that it is a product of mass culture and its consumption practices.

Folk culture can be easily incorporated in lifestyles; it is a quotable style for identity purposes. A folder advertising *Trachten* (adaptations of folk costumes) promises: "Living with tradition means to have a style which is above time." That is exactly the point: the newly-created accent on folk-regional culture promises timelessness in an ocean of temporality. It can claim timelessness because of its historical depth. Folk culture and culture suggest continuity and what is emphasized about them is that they are natural, invariant, deep-rooted and reliable. In search for timelessness, their borders as delineated in the national atlases of folk culture risk becoming interpreted as rigid distinctions, and thus usable as counterweights to mobility and the exacting demands of rapid changes.

Our analytical metaphors like "ethnoscapes" (Appadurai 1996) are only metaphors; we should take care not to exaggerate the differences and inadvertently to support the idea of ethnically-fashioned culture areas whose overdrawn distinctions can be used by less-scrupulous people, as in Yugoslavia. It cannot be by accident that in the newly-formed states of Croatia (Čapo-Žmegać 1998) and Slovakia (Stolicna 1997) recently volumes were published which describe their countries by means of their folk cultures, thus legitimating these states by their folkinesses but also in the worst case by deeply-rooted and irreconcilably-different ethnic "roots". Public folklore could be a useful part of our discipline: even if we do not realize it, we all practice "Public Folklore" (Welz 1996). At least some of us ought to reflect deliberately on this aspect of our business and ask what it is going to be used for, and by whom, here and abroad.

Our world is not merely a planet but a cosmos filled with meanings and senses which have already been set up by our predecessors, for instance by the practice of mapping cultural specialities (Zentai 1999: 70) like the national *Volkskunde-Atlas* did. The power of culture is going to overwhelm us if we cannot balance it. So, if it is true that we live in a *Kulturgesellschaft* (Lipp 1995) we have to reflect the power of what is called culture. It seems that the stories of the singularity and authenticity of local, regional or national culture fill in the gap and replace the state borders which people begin to miss, when the signs originally put up by state authorities begin to be taken down.

References

Altwegg, Jürg 1998: Blaues Wunder: Frankreich macht Ferien von der Geschichte. *Frankfurter Allgemeine Zeitung* August 25, 1988.

Appadurai, Arjun 1996: Disjuncture and Difference in the Global Cultural Economy. In: Arjun Appadurai, *Modernity at Large: Cultural Dimensions of Globalization*. Minneapolis, pp. 27–47.

Bendix, Regina 1997: *In Search of Authenticity: The Formation of Folklore Studies*. Madison, Wisconsin & London.

Byron, Reginald 1995: European Identities Transplanted across the Atlantic: The Irish-Americans of Albany, New York. *Ethnologia Europaea* 25:1, 33–44.

Čapo-Žmegać, Jasna et al. 1998: *Ethnografice: Svagdan i blagdan hrvatska puko*. Zagreb.

Elias, Norbert 1969: *Die höfische Gesellschaft: Untersuchungen zur Soziologie des Königtums und der höfischen Aristokratie* (= Soziologische Texte 54). Neuwied u.a., p. 17.

Ethnographia Bulgarica: Yearbook of Bulgarian Ethnology and Folklore. Sofia 1998.

Ethnologia Balkanica: Journal of Balkan Ethnology. Sofia 1997ff. (e.g., 1997, The Danube – a Bridge of Cultural Interchange).

Foucault, Michel 1970: *L'ordre du discours*. Paris. *(Die Ordnung des Diskurses*. München 1974.)

Froihofer, Waltraud 1998: Peter Roseggers Nachleben in der Waldheimat: Zur Situation in den Rosegger Gedenkstätten, den Rosegger-Vereinen und im touristischen Werbematerial. Dipl. Arb. Wien.

van Gennep, Arnold 1981: *Les rites de passage*. Paris.

Huntington, Samuel P. 1996: *The Clash of Civilizations*. New York.

International Symposium on the Occasion of the Fiftieth Anniversary of the Institute of Ethnology and Folklore Research, Zagreb. (= *Naroda Umjetnost* 36:1, 1999.)

Koppensteiner, Franz 1997: Kellergassen: Geschichte und Entwicklung. Dipl. Arb. Wien.

Köstlin, Konrad 1977: Das Essen und das Eigene. *Erziehung heute* e.h. 2, 7–11.

Köstlin, Konrad 1979: Anmerkungen zur kulturellen Identität von Deutsch-Amerikanern. *Kieler Blätter zur Volkskunde* 11, 77–100.

Köstlin, Konrad 1996: Perspectives of European Ethnology. *Ethnologia Europaea* 26, 169–189.

Köstlin, Konrad 2000: Roots, Rituals and Ethnicity as Metaphors. In: Regina Bendix & Herman Roodenburg (eds.), *Managing Ethnicity: Perspectives from Folklore Studies, History and Anthropology*. Amsterdam 2000, pp. 1–11.

Lipp, Wolfgang 1995: Kulturgesellschaft – was, und wohin? *Kultursoziologie* 4:2, 7–26.

Lübbe, Hermann 1981: *Zwischen Trend und Tradition: Überfordert uns die Gegenwart?* Zürich.

Magris, Claudio 1993: *Triest – eine literarische Hauptstadt in Mitteleuropa*. München.

Rihtman-Auguštin, Dunja 1998: Kroatien und der Balkan: Volkskultur – Vorstellungen – Politik. *Österreichische Zeitschrift für Volkskunde* 52:101, 151–168.

Senker, Gertraud 1998: Die "Mostarrichi"-Region: Über regionale Identität und das Entstehen von neuen Regionen im Rahmen des "Europas der Regionen". Dipl. Arb. Wien.

Sonna, Birgit 1998: Die alten Grenzen sind gefallen. *Süddeutsche Zeitung* June 12, 1998.

Spranger, Eduard 1953: *Der Bildungswert der Heimatkunde*. 2nd ed. Stuttgart.

Stolicna, Rastislava a.o. (eds.) 1997: *Slovakia: European Contexts of the Folk Culture*. Bratislava.

Turner, Victor 1982: *From Ritual to Theatre: The Human Seriousness of Play*. New York.

Welz, Gisela 1996: *Inszenierungen kultureller Vielfalt. Frankfurt am Main und New York City* (= Zeithorizonte 5). Berlin.

Zacharias, Wolfgang 1990: *Zeitphänomen Musealisierung: Das Verschwinden der Gegenwart und die Konstruktion der Erinnerung*. Essen.

Zentai, Violetta 1999: The *West* Envisions the West: Images of the Western World in Hungarian Critical Thought between the Two World Wars. *Ethnologia Europaea* 29:1, 69–84.

Konrad Köstlin is Professor emeritus at the Department of European Ethnology, Vienna University, Austria. The interplay and not so much the conflict between modernisation and the ongoing importance of ethnology and folklore (*Volkskunde*) – in terms of cultural analysis of everyday life and also as a provider of knowledge – can be seen as one accent in his work. Results, called culture or heritage and their impact as an argument within the formation of identity-games, are part of the current re-nationalisation of our world.
(konrad.koestlin@univie.ac.at)

THE CONCEPT OF (POST)IDENTITY IN QUEER AND MIGRATION STUDIES

Learning from Kira Kosnick

Silvy Chakkalakal, University of Basel

As a student, I was very interested in how people live together, how they make sense of the world, and how and why they organize their lives the way they do. Fascinated by the little things, the minor matters, the taken-for-grantedness of everyday life, European ethnology turned out to be the right place for me. Issues of racism, of social justice, the impact of social categorizing, power and knowledge as well as the possibilities of resistance and appropriation – all of these brought up burning questions. Back then, my studies were clearly driven by a desire to understand my own positioning in the world. European ethnology offered me classes on media practices and representation, on counter- and subcultures, on how people organize their leisure activities – the whole range of everyday life practices. And exactly this variety of topics also made *Ethnologia Europaea* as an interdisciplinary platform of cultural analysis an important resource for me. I always saw it as a journal presenting not only diverse research material, but also providing a space where international scholars have the possibility to reflect on theoretical, methodological, and political issues. Thus, from a wide range of significant articles that I might have chosen, I picked one that had an effect on me, and epitomizes this possibility for reflection.

Kira Kosnick's piece discusses the theoretical, methodological, and political predicaments of the concept of cultural identity. In her ethnographic study about the monthly party event *Gayhane* in the famous club SO36 in Berlin Kreuzberg, she writes about queer migrant clubbing and the production of semi-public urban spaces. Here, she shifts attention from identities to socialities; in so doing, she points out that especially within migration studies, classic approaches to identity tend to freeze people's subject positions within a classificatory system. The focus on sociality – that is forms of cultural practice and social engagement – instead offers a much more complex picture of group affiliations, relationships, and interactions. In her study about *Gayhane*, Kosnick concludes that looking at how

> different forms of sociality and association arise [...] is the very antithesis to the notion of community [as a locus of identity] that always already knows who and what it is speaking of – the "Turkish community", the "gay community" and so on. There is no pre-constituted group here, no pregiven solidarity that can be assumed, no predetermined way of life that seeks preservation, celebration, or integration into the wider imagined consensus of "society". (Kosnick 2008: 28)

We find in this article a double critique: firstly, she detects the reduction of identity to a mere signifier of ethnic and geographical belonging; secondly, she criticizes the reduction of the social to mere structural data such as crime, income statistics, educational performance and diplomas, or unemployment. In

Silvy Chakkalakal 2017: The Concept of (Post)Identity in Queer and Migration Studies: Learning from Kira Kosnick
Ethnologia Europaea 47:1, 65–68. © Museum Tusculanum Press.

her view, "the social" is characterized by diverse social practices and social affiliations and needs to be connected analytically with forms of cultural expression. By employing the concept of "migrant socialities" (ibid.: 24), she manages to combine these two spheres. Kosnick's evaluation of cultural identity goes even further when she calls for a less static understanding of classificatory categories such as ethnic background, gender, and sexual orientation. Yet, at the same time she does not neglect the possibility and ongoing struggle of doing politics from an identitarian position. Instead, she understands self-identification such as "being queer", "being Turkish", or "being people of color" as flexible and fluid, taking into account the many important interventions of postcolonial critics within the anthropological field (e.g. Moraga & Anzaldúa 1983; Abu-Lughod 1991; Palmié 2006; Bhabha 1994). Thus, Kosnick's article stands in the tradition of an ongoing debate inspired by theories of poststructuralism and postmodernity on the concept of identity, which fascinated and inspired me as a student reading postcolonial, migration, and queer studies.

In 2001, just two days before 9/11, I arrived in London to begin my year abroad studying media and cultural studies at Middlesex University. Xenophobia, racism, and institutionalized and everyday discrimination had never been purely theoretical issues to me and my student peers, but after 9/11 they became even more obvious and frequent. The political atmosphere in London changed drastically. Racist media representations, hate crimes, right-wing political initiatives, and increasingly intense debates over immigration provided students and professors with a constant flow of dreadful material. To many, it was clear that a discipline such as European ethnology or cultural studies needed to engage in this discussion, to talk back and to provide theoretically informed counter-narratives. Like many of my fellow students, I visited numerous events and talks, became part of a student activist group, heard scholars like Stuart Hall or Chantal Mouffe taking a stand against racism and islamophobia. One of the big questions we discussed constantly was how to deal with the concept of cultural identity. On the one hand, it seemed to be a tool used by people to express their belonging to a group; situating oneself in categories such as ethnicity, nationality, social class, gender, sexual orientation, or religion seemed almost like a natural thing to do. On the other hand, however, these very categories, as we were learning as students of "culture", were highly contested constructs. And didn't a climate like the one we experienced post-9/11 show that depending on such constructs for political organizing was a dangerous thing, as it was so clear that those very same categories were being used to exclude and oppress? Shouldn't we much rather reject engagement in a politics of identity that somehow, and often far too easily, concealed the historicity of the categories it depended on?

Kosnick's article makes this dilemma very vivid: How can we investigate and understand self-articulations in the form of identity concepts without relying on them methodologically? The predicament here is how to take the informant's identity expressions seriously, but at the same time not use the invocations of identity as an analytical concept. In the field of migration studies, for example, identity can often function too quickly as a transcendent essence, which puts people together in groups, be they nations, ethnicities, or any other kind of migrant social typology, such as the constant and problematic use of "community" shows:

> Instead, the concept of community carries with it the conceptual baggage it has been burdened with ever since the founding father of German sociology, Ferdinand Tönnies, posited it as a premodern, "organic" form of social grouping that predates the rise of modern society (Tönnies [1887]1912). Tight-knit bonds, shared genealogy, clearly defined membership, temporal continuity and lack of individual autonomy are the most prominent elements of what Tönnies and later Max Weber have described as the features of community as a basic type of social formation (Weber [1922]1980). (Kosnick 2008: 23)

Kosnick's article invites us to think about the dialectic between personal and group identity in the context of ethnographic research. The correlation between the two is again not only a social phenomenon we observe in the field, but also an epistemological one, since cultural analysts must synthesize their empirical observations with the help of analytical categories. In other words, the actions and articulations of the individual will have to be transferred into a bigger picture such as nation state, community, scene, subculture, etc. In my research on early ethnographic practices during the eighteenth-century anthropologization of the senses (Chakkalakal 2016), I have explored how early ethnographic images (e.g. copper plates, drawings, and sketches) of the cultural "Other" do the work of synthesizing empirical comparisons and observations. Early ethnographers understood these visual categorizations as causalities within cognitive processes: They functioned as evidence of important, indeed essential, knowledge that directly addressed the senses. Images of foreign people had to be true to the original, because otherwise the viewer would be in danger of falsifying the causal chains of knowledge production and their content. In the same way, Kosnick's critique of identity-focused approaches opens up the space for a reflective analysis of the methods and practices of ethnography itself and its political investments.

One might think that queer migrant clubbing is a marginalized cultural practice on which empirical research cannot offer sufficient insight into urban spaces as a whole. Kosnick's explanations of how this semi-public urban space is constituted contradicts such skepticism, allowing us to draw conclusions about other such spaces. The figure of the "queer migrant clubber" trespasses certain hegemonic orders such as heteronormativity or whiteness. As border crossers, they constantly disturb and subvert these hegemonic categories, and, by doing so, signify and affirm those very boundaries of the classificatory system, as Kosnick shows by putting the cultural practice of the clubbers, party organizers, and DJs in relation to mainstream categorical ordering. "Queer" or "Turkish" are therefore not to be understood as exceptional cases, but instead as part of a broader social order, which requires constant acts of boundary crossing for the very boundary to be marked.

Since Kosnick's article appeared, much has happened in the fields of queer and migration studies. In particular, the concept of postmigration has led to an approach that understands migration as a perspective of research rather than an object of research (e.g. Yildiz & Hill 2015; Bojadžijev & Römhild 2014). The shift from migrants to migration as a perspective stems from the above discussed problems with identity, and touches on the very notion of the subject itself. These are essential developments in theorizing and reformulating concepts of identity. Yet, in my opinion, we need to further investigate the subjective qualities attached to this, such as standpoint, voice, and experience (on the concept of experience see Chakkalakal 2014). These are all terms that lie at the operational heart of the social and cultural sciences. Even though Kosnick is not proclaiming we get rid of the concept of identity, she nevertheless calls for careful investigation of our methodological and epistemological research practices, which often derive from such seemingly self-evident concepts and therefore cement the very categories they want to contest. The "post" in postcolonial, postidentity, or postmigration does not mean a mere temporal "after", it does not follow a simple logic of "then" and "now". Instead, it signifies what has come into being in and through colonial, identitarian, and migratory relations and, at the same time, calls for a reconfiguration of the discursive fields and material structures in which these very categories "make sense".

In the end, what I have taken from Kosnick's article is a valuable culture-analytical attitude, which offers a vantage point for historical and ethnographic research in general: It is concerned with a reflective analysis of the classifications and concepts used by the social and cultural sciences. Taking people and their living conditions seriously means not to essentialize them by freezing "I", "you", "them", and "us" into epistemological models such as identity, individuality, and subjectivity. Having said this, we can inarguably observe identity in practice, for example in the form of an ethnographic "I". My own biographical framing of this text in the narrative form of a self-disciplinary (hi)story of a European ethnologist is the best example. In this light, subjectivity and identity need to be understood as open, dynamic, and in never-ending processes of emergence. These processes are not fully controlled and do not exhaust themselves in being reflective; instead they are haunted by a (disciplinary, political, epistemological) history and a future which are neither "mine", "yours", "theirs", or "ours". By reflecting on *Ethnologia Europaea*'s history, "I" as a writing and commenting scholar take up, inherit, transform, and become part of that history. According to the philosopher Daniel Dennett, the self is more of a "function" than it is a "source": "Our tales are spun, but for the most part we don't spin them; they spin us. Our human consciousness, and our narrative selfhood, is their product, not their source" (Dennett 1991: 418). It has been a great pleasure for me to merge narratively, biographically, and commentatorily into this great journal's history, and I thank the editors for giving me the opportunity.

References

Abu-Lughod, Lila 1991: Writing against Culture. In: Richard G. Fox (ed.), *Recapturing Anthropology*. Santa Fe: School of American Research Press, pp. 137–162.

Bhabha, Homi 1994: *The Location of Culture*. London: Routledge.

Bojadžijev, Manuela & Regina Römhild 2014: Was kommt nach dem "transnational turn"? Perspektiven für eine kritische Migrationsforschung. *Berliner Blätter* 65, 10–24.

Chakkalakal, Silvy 2014: Lebendige Anschaulichkeit: Zur Anthropologisierung der Sinne im 18. Jahrhundert. *Zeitschrift für Volkskunde* 110:1, 33–64.

Chakkalakal, Silvy 2017 (forthcoming): Indienliebe: Die frühe Ethnographie und ihre Bilder. Berlin: Kulturverlag Kadmos.

Dennett, Daniel C. 1991: *Consciousness Explained*. Boston: Little, Brown.

Kosnick, Kira 2008: Out on the Scene: Queer Migrant Clubbing and Urban Diversity. *Ethnologia Europaea* 38:2, 19–30.

Moraga, Cherríe & Gloria E. Anzaldúa (eds.) 1983: *This Bridge Called My Back: Writings by Radical Women of Color*. Latham, NY: Kitchen Table, Women of Color Press.

Palmié, Stephane 2006: Creolization and its Discontents. *Annual Review of Anthropology* 35, 433–456.

Tönnies, Ferdinand (1887)1912: *Gemeinschaft und Gesellschaft*. Berlin: Karl Curtius.

Weber, Max (1922)1980: *Wirtschaft und Gesellschaft*. 5. edition. Ed. by Johannes Winckelmann. Tübingen: Mohr.

Yildiz, Erol & Marc Hill (eds.) 2015: *Nach der Migration: Postmigrantische Perspektiven jenseits der Parallelgesellschaft*. Bielefeld: transcript.

Silvy Chakkalakal, Ph.D., is a senior researcher at the Institute of Cultural Anthropology and European Ethnology, University of Basel. Her research interests are anthropology of the senses, history of science of the eighteenth and nineteenth centuries, postcolonial theory, pictorial science, futurology, history of education and childhood studies. Her most recent publication is in press: Indienliebe: Die frühe Ethnographie und ihre Bilder (Berlin: Kadmos Verlag, 2017).
(silvy.chakkalakal@unibas.ch)

OUT ON THE SCENE
Queer Migrant Clubbing and Urban Diversity

Reprinted from *Ethnologia Europaea* 38:2, 2008

Kira Kosnick

This article develops a critique of identity-focused approaches to ethno-cultural diversity in urban settings by shifting attention from categorical identities to the question of socialities. Taking the example of a queer migrant club night as its point of departure, it shows how a focus on the forms of social engagement that are particular to migrant club scenes can contextualize identity claims but also go beyond them by highlighting the complexity of shifting affiliations and interactions that makes for the appeal of such scenes. Rather than seeing queer migrant club scenes as a protected refuge for a doubly discriminated minority, the consideration of socialities allows to reveal their functioning as semi-public urban formations.

Keywords: urban socialities, sexuality, ethnicity, diversity, leisure

The setting is Berlin Kreuzberg, late-night Saturday, with scores of people queuing down the block hoping to eventually make their way past the club doors in order to join the party. Over the course of an average *Gayhane* club night, more than one thousand people will have joined in, dancing to a mix of Turkish pop music with tunes from the Balkans, Israel, and translocal sounds between Hyderabad and London thrown in. The musical mix reflects its audience – not just in terms of its migrant origins, but in terms of its sexual ambiguities and gender expressions as well. The *Gayhane* club night has been created as an event to predominantly attract a 'queer'[1] Turkish-German crowd, though the party has become immensely popular among self-identified 'straight' Turkish-German clubbers. Queers without migrant backgrounds and other aficionados of Turkish pop music complement the picture, to form what enthusiastic journalists at Berlin's public-service radio station *Radio MultiKulti* and other media reporting have invariably termed something along the lines of a 'colourful celebration of diversity' or a 'multicultural paradise'. Other reports have instead stressed the functioning of *Gayhane* as a place of refuge for a doubly discriminated minority community: one that has a tough standing both in heteronormative Turkish environments and in a gay and lesbian scene in Berlin that entails different forms of racism.

The above paragraph more or less colludes with such mass media descriptions of *Gayhane* as a context of self-chosen urban diversity, naming as it does the dominant cultural schemes of classification that are linked to identity categories usually associated with such diversity: gender, sexual orientation, ethnic background. This article, however, tries to problematize this understanding of diversity, an understanding that is dominant not just in media reporting but also in academic approaches, by shifting attention from the problem of identity to one of sociality. What happens – theoretically, methodologically, politically – when we try to pay attention not to the categorical identities, claimed and ascribed, of the *Gayhane* crowd, but to the forms of sociality that are produced there? What if the interesting aspect of the event is not its classificatory composition, but what actually happens in terms of engagements between people in and around the club space?

Gayhane, I argue in the following, offers a good example of how a reductive understanding of the social and an exclusive focus on identity categories can blind us to the crucial social dynamics of a phenomenon. Club scenes like *Gayhane* point to different processes of sociality that rarely emerge in classical research on the social parameters of migrant and minority life. But neither do they emerge in culturalist, identity-focused perspectives that often neglect the question of the social altogether.

In the Mix

In the ten-year successful history of the club night, achieving the right 'mix' of the *Gayhane* audience has not been left to chance. Quite the contrary, its organizers have had to be continually concerned with what they have perceived as various audience imbalances and their related threats. Intended as a space in which queers with particular immigrant backgrounds would dominate, if not in numbers then at least in spirit, *Gayhane* functions as a public event, not as a club with restricted membership. Welcoming the participation of non-queers and non-immigrants, organizers have nevertheless had to contend with problems related to the shifting attraction of different audiences over the course of *Gayhane*'s existence. Having moved to Berlin in 1998 after several extended spells of living and working in Turkey's largest city Istanbul, a time during which I was active in the local Lambda organization and became part of queer transnational friendship circles that included some *Gayhane* organizers, I witnessed the different phases and dynamics of the club night as a regular visitor and friend.

During the first few years, it was the growing presence of gay men without immigrant backgrounds that was seen to threaten the character of the event. Attending the club night had become hip in certain non-immigrant gay circles, and many visitors with immigrant backgrounds began to feel uncomfortable with the former's orientalist expectations of finding certain kinds of erotic encounters in its wake. The door policy was adapted accordingly, in order to ensure that the main target group could still feel comfortable and not be pushed out. A few years later, the problem had transformed into one of securing the queer character of the *Gayhane* club night. This had partly to do with the fact that straight-identified Turkish-German and Kurdish-German women had discovered *Gayhane* as a place where they could dance to music they liked and enjoy themselves without the unwanted attention of men. However, it was just these self-identified straight men that began to attend in larger numbers once the women were there.

While straight-identified people had once attended because of their connection to members of the queer *Gayhane* audience, the club night increasingly attracted a straight clientele that in parts had little sympathy or tolerance for queers. Homophobic, sexist and especially transphobic incidents and violence in and outside the club space threatened to bring *Gayhane* to an end. After some discussion, the organizers responded by simultaneously trying to limit the access of straight-identified people, and starting an alternative Turkish club night that was not queer in character. *Hahane*, as the party was called, lasted merely a few months – not a single night passed without violent incidents,[2] and thus the organizing team discontinued the party. It had served its original partial purpose, though, in the sense that some pressure was taken off the *Gayhane* nights. Door policies are still in place today, however, to make sure that those entering the club space are mostly queer-identified.

An Eye for It

Various strategies have been employed to secure this composition inside the club, but most of the burden rests with the staff at the door. It is indeed partly a matter of categorical identifications here that determines the practical task at hand, and while gender expression and immigrant backgrounds can more easily be 'read off' the phenotypical/stylistic appearance of people in the queue,[3] finding out if someone fits the queer profile is a somewhat more difficult undertaking. Patricia, a lesbian African-German woman[4] who has worked at the door for years, told me:

> It gets incredibly difficult. But you can partly tell from their entire act, well, we are positioned pretty far outside, on the upper staircase. We look down the street and check out how people move about. Some of them show up, a heterosexual couple, smooching, to get in the queue and then to claim that they are gay and lesbian when they get to the door. And then I say, right, I can see that. Go to some other club. Or how someone behaves more generally, the way they gesture, how they walk, join in conversations and such. With guys, you can easily find out this way, in my opinion, how they interact with each other. With women it can be more difficult, but whoever comes along extremely done up, well, I'm sorry. (Kosnick 2005: 128)

Rather than simply relying on dominant cultural schemes of classification that associate gays and lesbians with stereotypical types of appearance and behaviour, discernable to a 'knowing' gaze, Patricia also refers to forms of perception that relate to particular queer sensibilities and cultural competencies. Being able to sense if someone shares queer identifications and/or desires is a crucial (and sometimes life-saving) competence for queers, especially in heteronormative environments, requiring the ability to pick up on subtle forms of comportment, of voice modulation, of self-presentation and aesthetics, of gait and attentiveness that easily go unnoticed by non-queers. These competences should of course not be assumed to share the same interpretive 'vocabulary' across different geopolitical and cultural spaces and contexts, as if queer subjectivities and practices were uniform in their expressive and communicative dimensions (Fortier 2002).

Yet, it is crucial to note here that this assessment of other people's queerness (as identification and/or desire) does not simply operate with dominant stereotypical indicators of classification. What in the Anglo-American context is often referred to subculturally as 'gaydar', a blending of 'gay' and 'radar' that has come to stand for the intuitive assessment of another person's queer identification or interest, entails multiple overlapping codes and sensory competences for different queer subcultures (Halberstam 2005), but most certainly differs from dominant stereotypical categorizations in terms of interpretive sophistication and intent. Importantly, assessment tends to involve more than observation, such as making eye contact and holding someone's gaze for a few seconds longer than a casual glance would warrant (Nicholas 2004). This form of assessment is also an act of engagement – the mutuality of a gaze that provides the basis for recognition – and thus always involves a form of minimal contact, and not simply of identification/categorization. The reciprocated gaze constitutes a form of interaction, and reveals in the mutuality of recognition something about the person who seeks the eye contact, not only about the person that meets and sustains the interaction.

This last method of assessment is of course of limited use to members of the door staff, who are easily identified by those who queue as gatekeepers in a literal sense. But Patricia and her colleagues use other forms of engagement as well if they are unsure as to a person's 'queer factor'. Engaging people in conversation provides an additional communicative terrain to interpret cues. 'So first you test it, a couple of questions, if you are not sure, start a conversation.' The best question to ask is not always the most direct one, Patricia states, such as asking whether people were gay or lesbian. '… the problem is that lots of people are not out there, and they still have a hard time to name it.' While the underlying assumption that there is a definite 'it' to be named and the expectation that there should be a temporal progression towards a naming can certainly be criticized (see Fortier 2002), what emerges here is a recognition that sexual practices and desires cannot be translated directly into modes of self-constitution and -presentation. Conversely, 'passing'[5] as queer can and does take place at the *Guyhane* door, but given that self-identified straight people rarely encounter situations that require explicit forms of dissimulation with regard to their sexual orientation, this is likely to happen less frequently than with queer-identified people in heteronormative clubbing environments. Less practice, less exigency. The border between queer and straight does not look the same from either side of the divide.[6]

Migrant Identities

Noting that the processes of identification at the club door involve complex forms of engagement and interpretation rather than just stereotypical categorizations on the part of staff members offers an opportunity to ground identity claims and ascriptions in the context of concrete communicative practices and performative action. Such contextualization, despite the well-rehearsed contemporary claims across academic disciplines that identities are always somehow constructed, occurs surprisingly rarely in the growing body of literature investigating the cultural identifications of migrants and their descendents across the social sciences and humanities.

What is at stake in this literature is most often the issue of ethnic, national or possibly diasporic identification, seen as an important indicator of cultural integration in countries of residence. With regard to academic work on second- or third-generation migrant youth in particular, older paradigms of young people 'being caught between two cultures' have given way to sophisticated discussions of cultural hybridity. Different intellectual and political precursors for this 'hybridity turn' in migration studies can be singled out, such as the anthropological critique of the culture concept in the 1990s (Abu-Lughod 1991), the earlier Caribbeanist and linguistic anthropology-led debates on creolization (see Palmié 2006), the postcolonial interventions of Bhabha and others (Bhabha 1994), and the feminist theorizations of intersectionality and location in the 1980s that problematized different axes of oppression (e.g. Moraga & Anzaldúa 1983).[7]

Questions of cultural identity have thus gained more prominence in migration studies, and continue to be fruitfully explored across different disciplines and in recently emergent trends towards transnationalist and diasporic approaches. A shared feature of many identity debates and studies, however, is what might be called a 'culturalist' concern with migrant orientations and identifications that focuses on the articulation and representation of migrants and diasporas in the context of cultural production (music, festivals, cultural organizations, media publications) or in the context of verbalized statements gathered as data in individual and group interviews. The latter provide probably the most widespread methodological tool to investigate questions of identity in migration studies today, not least because they tend to be easier to conduct than fieldwork methods that aim at examining the situated production of identity claims and cultural orientations in daily life contexts.[8] 'Culturalism' in migration studies has been described by anthropologists as the tendency to firmly tie back the ways in which migrants make sense of the world to an assumed cultural belonging that usually references nation-state origins (Çağlar 1990; Sökefeld 2004). The culprit in such accounts has usually been made out to be some form of cultural essentialism that reduces migrants to bearers of standard ethno-national qualities and proclivities.

However, it is not just cultural essentialism that feeds the culturalism of much work on migrant identities. It is also the common failure to situate the production of identity claims and ascriptions as part of social and institutional practices that contributes to culturalism, in the sense of separating identification as meaningful self- and other-description from their contexts of occurrence. The relevance, for example, of 'passing' as queer at the door of a Berlin nightclub would remain unintelligible without contextualizing it and explaining both why it is important and how a particular type of interaction unfolds. And it would be unlikely to even surface in research approaches that gather data on identity claims which are removed from concrete practices and events in migrants' lives. When people are asked to produce data/knowledge about themselves in the context of research interviews or surveys, their response will quite obviously be conditioned by the concrete demands and constraints of the informant situation. While this point seems hardly in need of pointing out to an ethnographically skilled audience, it is surprising how little critical reflection exists cross-disciplinary on the consequences of different methodological repertoires for researching migrant identifications. Instead, migrant articulations of cultural orientations and self-identifications are often taken as a form of evidence that exists in some kind of decontextualized state, simply to be verbalized whenever migrants are called upon to deliver statements for scientific perusal. As a consequence, the question of how such articulations are related to concrete social practices and engagements often cannot even arise (see Mannitz 2006).

Migrant Socialities

The considerable sophistication of current debates on the concepts of migrant culture and cultural identity has no parallel where the social dimensions of migrant lives are concerned, the ways in which migrants engage in social practices and form part of social formations. Possibly the most striking tribute to the poverty of the cross-disciplinary vocabulary when it comes to migrant socialities[9] is the notorious concept of community (Alleyne 2002; Amit & Rapport 2002). The community concept has come to function as a kind of placeholder for all kinds of migrant social groupings, and is endemic in both political debates and academic discourses. It is conveniently used to stand in for groupings produced through external classificatory practices – such as urban census measures that count the numbers of foreign nationals – and just as conveniently (if usually for quite different purposes) mobilized to support political-representational claims from 'within' minority groups, allowing such representatives to 'speak for' the group in question.

Glossing over the differences between the production of groups via classificatory practices and actual social-collective engagement can have various sorts of political effects, and not all of them negative.[10] Yet, what it precludes is any consideration of how different kinds of migrant sociality actually come into being, and what their relationship is to particular identity categories and claims. Instead, the concept of community carries with it the conceptual baggage it has been burdened with ever since the founding father of German sociology, Ferdinand Tönnies, posited it as a premodern, 'organic' form of social grouping that predates the rise of modern society (Tönnies [1887]1912). Tight-knit bonds, shared genealogy, clearly defined membership, temporal continuity and lack of individual autonomy are the most prominent elements of what Tönnies and later Max Weber have described as the features of community as a basic type of social formation (Weber [1922]1980). What are the implications, then, of the widespread standard formula by which migrant communities are taken to exist within particular societies, into which they integrate or not? It is a different form of essentialism that lurks here, one that links dominant schemes of classification to the assumption of an inescapable form of sociality, and is tinged with more than a hint of European social evolutionism (Stocking 1982) that associates non-European migrants with premodernity. It is striking that even quite sophisticated contemporary attempts to address questions of migration and identity in non-essentializing ways tend to take quick and unreflected recourse to the notion of community when referring to migrant social groupings.[11]

Efforts to demonstrate the malleability of cultural identifications are unfortunately rarely linked to examining the dynamics of social practices and emerging social formations. Dealing with the social is instead often left to the 'hard' social sciences that define migrant social parameters with regard to 'structural' data pertaining to labour markets, educational degrees, household statistics, residence patterns and the like. Levels of structural integration are then measured mostly by comparing quantitative information on educational performance, unemployment, crime and income statistics. The social life of migrants thus tends to be addressed only through the research prism of conventional institutions such as schooling, labour markets, family, or 'community' organizing on religious and ethnic grounds.[12]

The widespread differentiation between cultural integration on the one hand, referring to identifications and outlooks, and social integration on the other, measured via statistical data on structural factors, is in danger of sedimenting into an unfortunate division of labour – one in which the investigation of meaning production including identity claims, while seen as related to the analysis of social (read structural) factors, is taken to constitute a separate project. What easily disappears in the void between these divisions is any interest in the social beyond predictable structural categories. Instead of examining the relations between cultural expressions and diverse social practices that characterize migrants' lives, information on structural social factors is often provided only as static background information, separate from the analysis of identities and orientations.

The prevalent focus on 'structural' factors with regard to the social has dire consequences for the range and complexity of social forms and practices that can be considered relevant to migrants' lives. Practices that are not linked to formal institutions or leave traces that can be measured statistically by state agencies, academic or market surveys are much less likely to receive research attention.[13] Bruno Latour's scathing critique of what he calls the 'sociology of societies' (Latour 2005) can thus quite fruitfully be applied to the treatment of socialities in much contemporary migration research. By taking for granted what kinds of social structures are relevant to the study of migration, the question of just how migrants are involved in diverse practices and forms of social affiliation can no longer be asked. What would it mean, however, to try and posit the issue of migrant socialities as an open question?

Scenes of Club Culture

In the remainder of this article, I return to *Gayhane* and other migrant clubbing scenes in order to explore how a non-reductive understanding of the social could provide a different perspective on urban diversity. To repeat the question asked at the beginning, what happens – theoretically, methodologically, politically – when we try to pay attention not to the categorical identities, claimed and ascribed, of the *Gayhane* crowd, but to the forms of sociality that emerge in this context?

I became aware of this crucial distinction in the course of research at other Turkish club nights in Berlin, club nights where I tended to be one of very few visitors without a background from Turkey, as far as I could estimate. I conducted this research as a postdoctoral research fellow for the EU Fifth Framework Project 'Changing City Spaces: New Challenges to Cultural Policy in Europe'.[14] Carrying out comparative research on the impact of migration on cultural developments in a number of European metropolitan centres, our initial approach was mainly ethnocentric, in the sense that we focused on cultural developments that were closely related to particular immigrant groups that constituted important ethnic minorities within the respective cities. Seen from such an 'outside' analytical perspective, what seemed most interesting about most Turkish clubbing events was their apparent ethnically exclusive character – the fact that the vast majority of visitors seemed to share the same ethno-national background.[15] Could this be taken as an indicator of what in the German context has been dubbed *Parallelgesellschaften* (Worbs 2007), a development towards a more or less self-chosen form of immigrant segregation?

In the course of attending events and talking to visitors and organizers, it became clear that the ethnic composition of the audience was of very little concern to those involved. Organizers were far more concerned with attracting what they regarded as the right kind of target group as their audience, defining it with shifting emphases in terms of age, attitude, styling, 'class', and gender balance. While some organizers reflected upon the difficulties young immigrant men often used to have (and in places still have) when trying to get past the door at non-immigrant 'mainstream' clubs, and seeing this as a factor in the development of a Turkish-German club scene, the doors of their own clubs were by no means open to just anyone with the respective kind of ethno-national background: without proper attire – often meaning no trainers, hoodies etc. – and without female company, young men would still find themselves turned away at the door, albeit with different grounds for discrimination. Club audiences similarly described their scenes not in terms of ethnic criteria, but stressed factors such as age, attitude and style.

While these descriptions again hinge upon certain kinds of categorizations that have for other clubbing crowds been insightfully linked to (sub)cultural practices of distinction (Thornton 1995), they still cannot fully capture the allure that particular clubbing events hold for their respective audiences. What is it that makes for an exciting night out? While answers certainly differ across distinct groups of clubbers, one shared element emerged in the course of fieldwork that was rarely explicitly mentioned as such, yet invariably proved indispensible to the success of a club night in the implicit understandings of visitors and organizers.

I was attending a 'Sosyete' club night hosted at the *Oxymoron* venue in Berlin-Mitte, a sophisticated and relatively expensive club location in the heart of the gentrified city centre, when a young woman sat down next to me and we started talking. She said it was nice to see a new face, and she felt that this particular party was starting to get boring because it was always the same group of people who showed up. She was contemplating a change. What the young woman meant was not that she wanted more people without Turkish background there. She was merely making an observation that is key to the success of the vast majority of clubbing scenes: they lose their appeal once they fail to attract new visitors and lose their semi-public character. If you can no longer run into strange faces – the young woman thought and I agreed immediately – you might as well stay at home and invite your friends over. 'Going out' thus has to do with more than seeking the presence of particular kinds of people, it has to do with particular forms and possibilities of encountering strangers.

A clubbing scene is in this sense emphatically not about community, it is about particular kinds of urban publics. While it is nice to meet or run into people one knows when going clubbing, the 'kick' of going out has to do with these encounters taking place against the backdrop of an urban public that consists at least partially of strangers. Strangers with whom we might share a sexual orientation, gender expression or ethnic background, but people who are strangers none the less. They are most likely to remain strangers in the course of the night, but there are also all kinds of possibilities of encounter and social engagement. We might see through people, dance in their proximity, make eye contact, smile or talk to them, go home with them, and so on. The potential for specific encounters with strangers is what urban researcher Alan Blum has described as the essential quality and allure of urban scenes as contexts of selective association. While on the one hand, scenes are invariably specialized with regard to knowledge, taste, access and association, they simultaneously require a degree of openness in order to function:

> It sounds as if the scene confirms something about the associational life of the city, the ways its web of groups, societies and sects endow the city with a fraternal spirit, but this imagines the scene as a *Gemeinschaft*, whereas, in contrast, it is the mix of *Gemeinschaft-Gesellschaft* and their impossible reconciliation that makes for the lure and excitement of the scene. (Blum 2001: 20)

Scenes are neither purely intimate, exclusive social formations with clear-cut membership, nor accidental gatherings where people are thrown together anonymously and by and large unintentionally, to re-rehearse the two poles of community and society as defined by the founding fathers of German sociology. Youth researchers have described scenes as temporary forms of association that have a thematic focus, but a low degree of obligation and commitment (Hitzler 2003; Pfadenhauer 2005). For Blum, co-presence in a particular location and face-to-face encounters also form central elements of scenes, insofar as they thrive on the reciprocity of seeing and being seen:

> If public life invites us to enjoy being with others in an undemanding way, the public would be best conceived not as an incipient dialogue but as the erotic intensification of what is most intimate and exclusive that is produced by the activity of viewing and being viewed by the other. (Blum 2001: 24)

What interests Blum here is the social relationship that is produced in the mutuality of viewing in the context of scenes, one that might take quite different forms and carry various intentions, but always involves mutual engagement. The point is not to be a disinterested observer, but to participate, to make contact. Clubbing environments provide very particular contexts for social engagement with the carefully designed sensory stimulation they provide: the relative darkness, the level of noise which often renders verbal communication difficult, the close proximity of others, and the architectural design of spaces to dance, to sit, to mingle, to withdraw, to space out, to tune in. They thus encourage communication via eye contact and body movements, while offering ample room for experimentation and ambiguity: regarding the intentionality of moving into somebody's proximity, of casting a glance, of offering a smile, of copying dance moves, of brushing against someone. Often heightened via the consumption of various kinds of stimulants, different clubbing scenes and clubbers will seek to produce different sensory and emotional experiences, many of which might not be primarily oriented towards mutual engagement.[16] However, the 'scenic' forms of sociality provide a crucial context for these experiences, which are deliberately sought out in qualified public settings.

The importance of socialities rarely surfaces in interview-based data on people's clubbing habits. If asked why someone frequents a particular club night, respondents tend to refer to the same indicators – the hipness factor of people, the music, the venue. The social dimensions of their clubbing experience are much more likely to emerge in the context of participant observation, when different factors come to the fore: questions of how to present oneself to whom, where to go within the venue, what to do when and how to engage with whom. This is not to claim that participant observation offers transparent and authoritative access to ethnographic truths – observing as a sensory practice, method of object construction and knowledge production in anthropology obviously comes with its own heavy historical baggage, a baggage that has accumulated in the debates over the status of anthropology as a science and form of representation (Atkinson & Hammersley 1994). Rather, the point is to note that observation as a practice of world engagement and interpretation (Schürmann 2008) allows to pay attention to the nuances of situated and often non-verbal acts that tend to be screened out in other methodological repertoires.

Very interesting aspects emerge also when observing and engaging the experts on collective practice in the context of clubbing, the DJs. They are themselves the keenest observers of particular social dynamics within the vicinity of the dance floor, since they have to 'know' how their audience ticks in order to produce a positive dance experience and atmosphere. In many explicitly dance-oriented clubs, DJs try to build up a collective sense of excitement that has often been described as a 'tribal' or 'fraternal' spirit among frenzied dancers that can peak several times in the course of a successful DJ set (Lawrence 2003).

Noting the origins of modern dance club scenes in the social circles of queer ethnic/racial minority subcultures in the United States, Tim Lawrence has described how an underground club scene in the 1960s helped to create safe public spaces for queer socialities, for people whose supposed minority 'communities' offered anything but a place to belong (ibid.). While belonging was certainly a concern for some – important to note here is the emergence of so-called 'houses' that modelled themselves on extended family structures to offer binding social ties, practical help and solidarity to queer minority men (Zea 2000) – underground clubs thrived only when their audience functioned as a scene, with access limited to those in the know, but never restricted to a clearly demarcated group of people. It was not just about being in the presence of particular kinds of people but about engaging with them in different ways that made for the appeal of these clubs.

It would be highly reductive, then, to regard clubbing audiences merely as a group of people that have features in common such as age, musical taste, style, (sub)cultural capital, class positions, possibly ethnic backgrounds, gender expressions or sexual orientations. While Sarah Thornton has charged that club-cultural crowds '… generally congregate on the basis of their shared taste in music, their consumption of common media and, most importantly, their preference for people with similar tastes to themselves' (Thornton 1995: 200), this does not suffice to explain the social dynamics that characterize clubbing as event and club scenes as social formations. The dimensions of sociality that form part of clubbing events cannot be explained exclusively with reference to cultural schemes of classification or possibilities for cultural distinction, they have to be understood as properly social phenomena in their own right. An effort has to be made to understand how people actually engage with each other, and to describe the quality and dynamics of their affiliatory practices and the social formations they (re-)produce or transform.[17]

This point has similarly been made by critics of the subcultural studies paradigm developed out of the Birmingham school of cultural studies, where the study of youth subcultures formed an important focus for analyzing the cultural dynamics of class conflicts. Subcultures, David Muggleton has charged, are too often regarded as homogeneous and static systems, partly because the classical cultural studies approaches have primarily sought to determine their 'authenticity' with regard to a 'proper' class base rather than understanding their dynamic qualities (Muggleton 2005; see also Bennett 2003).

Conclusion

The implications of focusing on the social dimensions and dynamics of club scenes emerge with greater clarity when we return to the *Gayhane* club night and the perspectives that have been cast upon it as either multicultural paradise or protected refuge. The description of its history and the analysis of its door politics have shown that in some aspects *Gayhane* can be considered a protected space, but not as a communal refuge of a doubly oppressed minority.

Being identified as not conforming to heteronormative standards can often imply acute danger in urban public settings. Kissing one's partner or lover in public, a taken-for-granted privilege of heterosexual couples in many European metropolitan public spaces, can elicit various threatening and unwanted responses in those very same spaces for same-sex couples (Mason 2002). While queer club spaces offer relative protection from such responses, just as do non-homophobic 'private' spaces, it is not just protection but the public character of the environment that counts. *Gayhane* is not a safe haven, nor a 'homelike space' (Petzen 2004), it is foremost a qualified face-to-face public gathering. Being in the presence of strangers that find one's doings and appearance unremarkable or affirmative is, in fact, remarkable in this context, and quite a different experience than being part of a 'community' implies. It is here that the political implications of shifting attention from identity to sociality begin to emerge: what does it mean for visitors to participate in and experience public gatherings that are not heteronormatively coded? For those who find their desires, affections and identifications at odds with dominant heteronormative and ethno-national standards, the experience of 'queer' and 'oriental' publics might suggest a different potential for change than that afforded by the experience of community belonging.

People who go to *Gayhane* do not simply want to be among people like themselves. Their interest is rather to be in a queer and Turkish-identified space where it is possible to participate in qualified publics – in this case in publics where one's presence is *not* reduced to subordinated categories of identity. The point is that what is most noticeable from a dominant heteronormative and ethnically unmarked perspective – the queer 'oriental' classification – can move to the background for participants, precisely because it structures the space in the first place. In order to understand, though, that there is more to

Gayhane than happily mixed minoritarian identities, one has to pay attention to the social dynamics and qualities of the club night as a scene.

What does this tell us about urban diversity? Urban space does not automatically bring forth 'cross-fertilization' and mixing just by virtue of being home to diverse populations, diverse in the sense of ethnic or sexual categories. Neither does the mere spatial co-presence of people that can be classified along multiple categories of identity tell us much about how these people relate to each other in social terms. The urgent (political as well as academic) question is rather how different forms of sociality and association arise, and under what conditions – particularly with regard to different forms of public life (Warner 2002). That is the very antithesis to the notion of community that always already knows who and what it is speaking of – the 'Turkish community', the 'gay community' and so on. There is no pre-constituted group here, no pregiven solidarity that can be assumed, no predetermined way of life that seeks preservation, celebration, or integration into the wider imagined consensus of 'society'. Positing the issue of migrant socialities in urban spaces as an open question thus opens up a new terrain of inquiry: one that does not prioritize questions of identity but rather asks about social practices and forms of affiliation that tend to go unnoticed in the current division of labour between cultural and social sciences.

Notes

1 The term is used here to refer to sexual orientations as well as gender identifications and expressions that do not conform to heteronormative expectations.

2 Conflicts ensued mostly between straight men and without homophobic background, as far as I was told, and some of them appear to have been related to drugs.

3 These readings are of course anything but 'straight'forward, themselves mobilizing dominant and subaltern cultural schemes of classification that have been partially naturalized. At the *Gayhane* door, however, a failure to easily 'read' and categorize someone as either male or female will enhance rather than diminish that person's chances of being granted access to the club space.

4 Her own self-descriptive terms for the purpose of this discussion.

5 Passing has been described both for racialized and sexual minorities, whereby 'members' of oppressed minority groups successfully hide or manage not to disclose their minority status vis-à-vis dominant groups and institutions (Robinson 1994).

6 It is interesting here to draw a parallel between Frederik Barth's famous discussion of ethnic boundary maintenance and the case at hand (thanks to the anonymous reviewer for drawing my attention to this point). It was Barth's contribution to highlight the political character of ethnic identity in the context of constructing and maintaining boundaries and role differentiation between groups (Barth 1970). In this case, the very construction of 'queer' as other is a result of historically specific heteronormative paradigms that have used a variety of different mechanisms to produce subaltern subjects as deviant, unnatural, sick or immoral, without conceding the same visibility to 'heterosexual' as a category of identification. Given that the identification/construction of sexual minorities is in these constellations inseparable from various forms of violence and dominance, it might be more productive to compare (yet not liken) the maintenance and policing of normative heterosexuality to the policing of whiteness as invisible norm in certain historical contexts of racial politics, where different degrees of visibility and knowledge are attached to dominant and subaltern positions (Hartigan 2005; hooks 1992; Williams 1989).

7 Further non-academic factors that deserve mentioning involve for example the transformation of capitalist markets that increasingly rely on the circulation of signs (Lash & Urry 1994), and mobilize cultural processes of hybridization in the interest of an unlimited commodification of cultural differences (e.g. Nghi Ha 2005).

8 Various major studies of immigrant youth identities in Europe have relied and continue to rely on interview methods to gather their data (e.g. Vertovec & Rogers 1998; Heitmeyer et al. 1997; see Miller 2006).

9 I use this concept here in a wide sense to denote all forms of social engagement and affiliations between people.

10 There is no doubt that such forms of representational claims have been crucial to different kinds of emancipatory projects, for gay and lesbian politics as much as for 'racial' and ethnic minority empowerment. The downside is, of course, the instrumentalization of representational politics in the interest of non-emancipatory politics, such as when the British government calls upon the British Muslim 'community' to fight extremism in 'its' midst by reigning in its angry young men, whose occasional proclivity to become suicide bombers must surely be linked to educational failures in said 'community'.

11 Witness, for example, the use of the concept in the

2005 British Arts and Humanities Research Council programme specification for a new research initiative on diasporas, migration and identities, intended to produce cutting-edge research.

12 It would be too cumbersome here to try and provide a representative list of references for 'hard' social science approaches that work with the above-mentioned indicators.

13 There are, of course, very notable exceptions: the paradigm shift towards the study of transnational social formations and spaces, for example, has helped to unsettle engrained orthodox expectations regarding not just cultural orientations of migrants but also social practices and new institutions.

14 www.citynexus.com.

15 This is without regard here to the ethnic heterogeneity present among immigrants from Turkey, including but not limited to the Kurdish-Turkish divide.

16 It would be important here of course to look in more detail at specific drugs and their impact with regard to particular forms of sociability, noted for ecstasy as a drug of choice in rave and techno scenes, for crystal meth in gay sex party scenes, and so on (see Hitzler 2002; Slavin 2004).

17 This is not just a question of micro- and macro-approaches either, as might seem opportune from a sociology perspective that is used to treating questions of interpersonal engagement as a matter of micro-analysis, while treating 'structure' as a macro-affair. The 'structural' macro-approaches risk to miss out on precisely those social formations and dynamics that do not have a high degree of visibility, that cannot be easily demarcated, that seem ephemeral and fleeting.

References

Abu-Lughod, Lila 1991: Writing against Culture. In: Richard G. Fox (ed.), *Recapturing Anthropology*. Santa Fe: School of American Research Press, pp. 137–162.

Alleyne, Bryan 2002: An Idea of Community and its Discontents. *Ethnic and Racial Studies*, vol. 25, no. 4, 607–627.

Amit, Vered & Nigel Rapport 2002: *The Trouble with Community*. London: Pluto Press.

Atkinson, Paul & Martyn Hammersley 1994: Ethnography and Participant Observation. In: Norman K. Denzin & Yvonna S. Lincoln (eds.), *Handbook of Qualitative Research*. Thousand Oaks, CA: Sage, pp. 248–261.

Barth, Frederik (ed.) 1970: *Ethnic Groups and Boundaries: The Social Organization of Cultural Difference*. London: Allen and Unwin.

Bennett, Andy 2003: Researching Youth Culture and Popular Music: A Methodological Critique. *British Journal of Sociology*, vol. 53, no. 3, 451–466.

Bhabha, Homi 1994: *The Location of Culture*. London: Routledge.

Blum, Alan 2001: 'Scenes.' Janine Marchessault & Will Straw (eds.), *Public*, no. 22/23, 7 36.

Çağlar, Ayşe 1990: Das Kulturkonzept als Zwangsjacke in Studien zur Arbeitsmigration. *Zeitschrift für Türkeistudien* 3, 93–105.

Fortier, Anne-Marie 2002: Queer Diaspora. In: Diane Richardson & Steven Seidman (eds.), *Handbook of Lesbian and Gay Studies*. London: Sage, pp. 183–197.

Halberstam, Judith 2005: *In a Queer Time and Place*. New York & London: New York University Press.

Hartigan, John 2005: *Odd Tribes: Toward a Cultural Analysis of White People*. Durham & London: Duke University Press.

Heitmeyer, Wilhelm, Joachim Müller & Helmut Schröder 1997: *Verlockender Fundamentalismus: Türkische Jugendliche in Deutschland*. Frankfurt am Main: Suhrkamp.

Hitzler, Ronald 2002: Pill Kick: The Pursuit of 'Ecstasy' at Techno-Events. *Journal of Drug Issues*, vol. 32, no. 2, 459–465.

Hitzler, Ronald 2003: Jugendszenen: Annäherungen an eine jugendkulturelle Gesellungsform. In: Wiebken Düx, Thomas Rauschenbach & Ivo Züchner (eds.), *Kinder und Jugendliche als Adressatinnen und Adressaten der Jugendarbeit*. Dortmund (Jugendhilfe in NRW, H. 4), pp. 11–21.

hooks, bell 1992: *Black Looks: Race and Representation*. Boston: South End Press.

Kosnick, Kira 2005: Selecta at the Door: Queer 'Oriental' Space and the Problem of Getting the Mix Right at Gayhane Clubnights. *Berliner Blätter*, no. 37, 126–131.

Lash, Scott & John Urry 1994: *Economies of Signs and Space*. London: Sage.

Latour, Bruno 2005: *Reassembling the Social*. Oxford: Oxford UP.

Lawrence, Tim 2003: *Love Saves the Day: A History of American Dance Music Culture, 1970–1979*. Durham & London: Duke University Press.

Mannitz, Sabine 2006: *Die verkannte Integration*. Bielefeld: transcript Verlag.

Mason, Gail 2002: *The Spectacle of Violence: Homophobia, Gender and Knowledge*. London: Routledge.

Miller, Mark J. 2006: 'Opportunities and Challenges for Migrant and Migrant-background Youth in Developed Countries.' Report submitted to the United Nations Social and Economic Council, July 15.

Moraga, Cherry & Gloria Anzaldúa (eds.) 1983: *This Bridge Called My Back: Writings by Radical Women of Color*. Latham, NY: Kitchen Table, Women of Color Press.

Muggleton, David 2005: From Classlessness to Clubculture: A Genealogy of Post-war British Youth Cultural Analysis. *Young*, vol. 13, no. 2, 205–219.

Nghi Ha, Kien 2005: *Hype um Hybridität*. Bielefeld: transcript Verlag.

Nicholas, Cheryl 2004: Gaydar: Eye-gaze as Identity Recognition among Gay Men and Lesbians. *Sexuality and Culture*, vol. 8, no. 1, 60–86.

Palmié, Stephane 2006: Creolization and its Discontents. *Annual Review of Anthropology*, vol. 35, 433–456.

Petzen, Jennifer 2004: Home or Homelike? Turkish Queers Manage Space in Berlin. *Space & Culture*, vol. 7, no. 1, 20–32.

Pfadenhauer, Michaela 2005: Ethnography of Scenes. Towards a Sociological Life-world Analysis of (Posttraditional) Community-building. *Forum Qualitative Sozialforschung* [Online Journal]. http://www.qualitative-research.net/index.php/fqs/article/view/23/49, last accessed 20/08/07.

Robinson, Amy 1994: It Takes One to Know One: Passing and Communities of Common Interest. *Critical Inquiry*, vol. 20, no. 4, 715–736.

Schürmann, Eva 2008: *Sehen als Praxis: Ethisch-ästhetische Studien zum Verhältnis von Sicht und Einsicht*. Frankfurt am Main: Suhrkamp Verlag.

Slavin, Sean 2004: Drugs, Space and Sociality in a Gay Nightclub in Sidney. *Journal of Contemporary Ethnography*, vol. 33, no. 3, 265–295.

Sökefeld, Martin 2004: Das Paradigma kultureller Differenz. In: M. Sökefeld (ed.), *Jenseits des Paradigmas kultureller Differenz*. Bielefeld: transcript Verlag, pp. 9–33.

Stocking, George 1982: *Race, Culture, and Evolution: Essays in the History of Anthropology*. Phoenix edition, Chicago: University of Chicago Press.

Thornton, Sarah 1995: *Club Cultures: Music, Media and Subcultural Capital*. Cambridge: Polity Press.

Tönnies, Ferdinand (1887)1912: *Gemeinschaft und Gesellschaft*. Berlin: Karl Curtius.

Vertovec, Steven & Alisdair Rogers (eds.) 1998: *Muslim European Youth: Reproducing Ethnicity, Religion, Culture*. Aldershot: Ashgate.

Warner, Michael 2002: Publics and Counterpublics. *Public Culture*, vol. 14, no. 1, 40–94.

Weber, Max (1922)1980: *Wirtschaft und Gesellschaft*. 5. edition. Ed. by Johannes Winckelmann. Tübingen: Mohr.

Williams, Brackette 1989: A Class Act: Anthropology and the Race to Nation across Ethnic Terrain. *Annual Review of Anthropology*, vol. 18, 401–444.

Worbs, Susanne 2007: 'Parallelgesellschaften' von Zuwanderern in Deutschland? In: *Sozialwissenschaftlicher Fachinformationsdienst soFid*. http://www.gesis.org/information/sofid/pdf/Migration-2007-1.pdf, last accessed 12/04/2008.

Zea, Joel J. 2000: This is OUR House: The Rise and Fall of a Homosexual Institution. Senior Essay written at Wesleyan University. http://www.cundrie.com/engl01/sp2005/zea.pdf, last accessed 13/09/2008.

Kira Kosnick is Junior Professor of Cultural Anthropology and European Ethnology at Goethe University Frankfurt. She has recently published the monograph *Migrant Media: Turkish Broadcasting and Multicultural Politics in Berlin* (Indiana University Press, 2007) and co-edited *Islam auf Sendung* (together with Anke Bentzin et al., Dagyeli Verlag, 2007). Her current ERC research project 'New Migrant Socialities: Ethnic Club Cultures in Urban Europe' focuses on migrant club scenes and related social practices in London, Berlin and Paris.
(kosnick@em.uni-frankfurt.de)

Author's Comment on the Reprint

Reflecting back on the article that was written almost ten years ago, there are two issues that I would address differently if I had the chance. One pertains to the rather cheap dismissal of the Birmingham school of cultural studies, which did in fact contribute so much more to the study of subcultures than I allege in the article – most notably with Stuart Hall, Angela McRobbie and Paul Gilroy all having provided crucial interventions with regard to race and gender beyond and in articulation with class. Secondly, I would aim for a more complex discussion and use of the term queer, as my deployment too easily glosses over the different histories of activism and struggles around identities and politics in and across lesbian, feminist, transgender, intersex and gay male circles – histories and struggles that matter also in the context of nightlife that I have discussed in the article.

Kira Kosnick is now Professor of Sociology at Goethe University Frankfurt, and co-director of the university's Cornelia Goethe Center for Women and Gender Studies. She has expanded her work on sexuality and postmigrant nightlife scenes in the context of an ERC Starting Grant project, and in 2015 published some of the results in the book *Postmigrant Club Cultures in Urban Europe* (Frankfurt: Peter Lang).
(kosnick@em.uni-frankfurt.de)

RE-INVENTING AND DECONSTRUCTING EUROPE

All in 136 Centimetres

Comment for the Anniversary Issue

Orvar Löfgren, University of Lund

Down in the basements of the humanities library at Lund University I find 50 years of *Ethnologia Europaea*, tightly stacked. Even in this old analogue form, they take up surprisingly little space. Is this all, 136 centimetres?

Instead of leafing through them chronologically, I start diving in here and there. It works like a time machine, travelling back and forth through different eras of European ethnology. Sometimes it makes me a bit dizzy.

Looking at the first issues, I'm reminded that launching an international journal is always a big project. There are the tricky questions about funding, market, and audience, finding editors as well as picking an editorial board that balances different interests and stakeholders. Once the new ship starts sailing, it may turn out that it takes a course not planned or foreseen. Much energy is devoted to keep it afloat, struggling for subscribers, enough funding, and not least: good papers. For editors these daily tasks usually overshadow grander plans about "The Mission of Our Journal".

Ethnologia Europaea was very much started as a journal with a mission, an attempt to pull together all kinds of research activities and academic traditions under the umbrella of a nascent European ethnology. The journal was a tool for building a scholarly community and the carefully composed editorial board was essentially a club, which owned the project.

When Erixon wrote his introduction to this new project, he was 79 years old and died a year later. This was his final call. In her comment on his paper, Dorothy Noyes nicely captures the mood in which the journal was launched and the roads taken or not taken in the process. She points to Erixon as a *bricoleur* making do with the scarce resources available. Reading Erixon's paper I am struck by his constant effort to build cooperation and also his cautious navigation in the "geo-politics" of European ethnology (East and West, South and North). Another striking element is that of intergenerational differences. As in American folklore there were many young Turks mobilizing – demanding a new European ethnology. Actually, there were several generations of young Turks, the not so very young ones, who already in the late 1950s wanted to reinvent the discipline, and the very young ones we today associate with 1968 and the German "Abschied vom Volksleben". For many young scholars *Ethnologia Europaea* was seen as an old men's club. Back then, a colleague of mine said in a derogatory tone of the new journal: "too many papers on goat cheese making and a design that looks like something from the 1930s". *Ethnologia Europaea*

Orvar Löfgren 2017: Re-Inventing and Deconstructing Europe: All in 136 Centimetres. Comment for the Anniversary Issue
Ethnologia Europaea 47:1, 81–83. © Museum Tusculanum Press.

was held together not least by the European atlas projects, which still worked as a centripetal force. It was a Europe united by historical flows of farm buildings, tools, and traditions, by processes of innovation and diffusion, borders and cultural regions. In a sense it made Europe (or some aspects of it) very visible and material, in ways which later appeals for European cooperation and community-building has found it hard to do. On the other hand, the political concept of Europe was a very vague idea back in 1967 compared to the intense European debates of 2017.

Leafing through the journal, I am also struck by how the Europe of *Ethnologia Europaea* is constantly changing. Back in 1967, it was important to get every corner of the continent into the project, with reports on the situation from Albania to Lithuania. There are presentations of national ethnologies from 25 European countries in the first issue and during the first years, it is striking that there is a constant search for presentations of national research. Sometimes it makes for too much catalogue reading.

Ethnologia Europaea's history can also be read as the constant re-invention of Europe. A good example of this is found in Nevena Škrbić Alempijević's comments on Konrad Köstlin's paper "Vanishing Borders and the Rise of Culture(s)" from 1999. Both of them discuss the paradox that the making of European regions create boundaries and formulas which separate but on another level pulls Europe together. Different corners of the continent are made to stand out as special with the help of an intensely European tool box and check list.

From time to time, new *Ethnologia Europaea* conferences were arranged to discuss the Europeanness of European ethnology or possible paths of cooperation, but as the years pass, this European project is no longer so evident in the journal. Southern and Eastern Europe are less present in the 1980s and 1990s. And as English becomes the preferred language during the 1990s, the number of German and French contributions dwindle, at least for a number of years.

There are also other factors at play in this de-Europeanization of European ethnology. In the 1970s and 1980s, the discipline expanded in many places, attracting more students and resources, which helped create a more inward-looking national focus. Europe was not needed in the same way to promote the discipline. New dialogue partners were found in American and British social sciences.

Seeing all the earlier efforts of building a comparative European framework, I cannot help longing for some new attempts at a comparative or at least contrastive approach. Today, with all the agonies of the continent, one could start contemplating some kind of joint cooperation on issues like migration, re-nationalization, political nostalgia, and much more... And the comparative or contrasting approach does not have to take the form of large-scale projects, which might get lost in the bureaucratic jungles of EU funding. It can take the form of a dialogue across national borders, increasing awareness that European ethnology is the same over there, but also different in challenging ways.

In a sense, the thematic issues of *Ethnologia Europaea* often take the form of such a European dialogue. Peter Jan Margry discusses my contribution to the thematic issue of "The Nationalization of Culture" back in 1989. Rereading that issue, I remember how important it was for us Scandinavians to go to Budapest in the 1980s to get a new perspective on the tensions of the national project in a totally different political setting. Suddenly, our notion of national identity seemed naïve or at least very provincial. Looking back, I can see many of the thematic issues as low-budget but creative forms of European cooperation, which one does not find as often in other journals in the field. This is an *Ethnologia Europaea* tradition to keep up.

Leafing through 136 centimetres of *Ethnologia Europaea*, I am struck by the richness of topics and breadth of contributors, not only from different countries but different disciplines. The choices of papers and the comments on them mirror this, but there is also the fun of revisiting earlier research, old contributions, which appear in new light. And some turn out to have strong staying power, for example Kira Kosnick's paper on queer migrant clubbing, which Silvy Chakkalakal shows addresses important issues of urban sociability and the problems of identity politics, which are still with us.

In her comment, Martine Segalen notes how trends and foci come and go in *Ethnologia Europaea*. As a former editor I can now, in retrospect, see the selectivity that was hidden from my view at the time. Each editor (including myself) has his or her favourite approaches, topics, scholars. Bjarne Stoklund needs a special salute for his bridging of generational and national differences during his long stint as editor.

As I carry the stacks back to the shelves – what have I learned? In one of the early issues, the editor makes an excuse for introducing an overview of an older scholar's work – presented as someone not very fashionable for contemporary ethnology, but the editor goes on to say that it is not a bad idea to return and take a retrospective look at a research tradition. Diving in and out of volumes, I am reminded of the old saying that in European ethnology, one can write about practically anything. However, this freedom comes with a distinctive style of doing research, which holds the discipline together. Even goat cheese studies return in the 2000s, but now as a part of an analysis of gastronomic politics of European regions and "terroir". And, in *Ethnologia Europaea* 2014 (44:2) two young scholars revisit the atlas project my generation loved to ridicule to discuss new potentials for mapping as an analytical strategy.

A couple of hours spent leafing through the journal issues taught me a lot. In a way, it was a quicker path to understanding the constantly changing modes and moods of doing European ethnology than reading heavy tomes of disciplinary history. As Regina Bendix discusses in her comment, there are constant processes of ageing and rejuvenating going on.

Finally, I was struck by the many surprises hiding in the volumes and the ways in which authors still are allowed to experiment, not only with topics, but with forms and styles. There is a rapid current streamlining of academic journals going on, as big publishing factories develop assembly lines, with tight rules, digital templates, and outsourcing of editorial work. There is a constant trend towards standardization of papers and peer reviews (again more templates), often imitating the traditions of "hard" social-science writing. The result is often a too predictable format (introduction, formulation of problems, previous research, empirical materials, analysis... etc.). In this light, *Ethnologia Europaea* still stands out as an open and informal journal and these are qualities that should be safeguarded. I would love for the journal to continue to give space to ethnographic experiments, the mixes of text and images, crazy ideas, and non-conformist approaches. Now there's a challenge for the future!

Orvar Löfgren, Professor emeritus in European Ethnology at the Department of Cultural Sciences, Lund University, Sweden. The cultural analysis and ethnography of everyday life has been an ongoing focus in his research. Central research fields have been studies of national identity and transnational mobility, media and consumption.
(orvar.lofgren@kultur.lu.se)

SHE GROWS YOUNGER EVERY YEAR...

Comment for the Anniversary Issue

Regina F. Bendix, Georg-August-University Göttingen

Ideally, a scholarly journal is constantly running ahead of its time. Sketching plans for a future, gently or not so gently revising extant perspectives, introducing topics holding promise for a field to unfold: such can be the tasks of editors striving to keep a journal abreast of intellectual developments in a field. Editors age in the process, scouting for good submissions, prodding peer reviewers, and juggling production schedules. But the journal grows younger, provided authors venture to send in material that has this potential. There are, of course, the disciplinary checks and balances: not all adventuresome submissions survive the peer-review process and some surface at the other end of revise and resubmit chastened and adjusted to peers' expectations. There may also be phases of consolidation where sound scholarship is what appears in issue after issue, exemplifying the best the field has to offer. But perhaps such phases might better be termed years of gathering strength toward casting off another skin, only to emerge with shiny new scales, glittering or bristling, arousing joy, curiosity, and irritation and thus moving the field forward, growing younger all the while. If a journal did not succeed in this opposite course to aging, it would slowly but surely lose its readership.

Authors and scholars, like editors, are subject to aging. Their minds may be flexible, hanging on to the capacity to identify a new turn, another paradigm shift, by their own insatiable curiosity and – assisted by eager, emerging young dissertation writers – they may stay abreast of what is passé and what is up and coming. We may suppress that recognition in the daily business of teaching and administering. But given the opportunity occasioned by this issue, to peruse a decade of *Ethnologia Europaea* and choose one article to reflect on in detail, many of the contributors opted to insert autobiography and take a few steps on memory lane – thus invariably acknowledging transitions and transformations within both the discipline and the self, all the while also identifying lasting cores. Martine Segalen, considering Liv Emma Thorsen's contribution on work and gender from the 1986, writes "I must confess that there might also be some nostalgia on my part, considering the fact the rural household as a socio-anthropological domain is no longer *à la mode*." Out of this nostalgia she simultaneously generates appreciation for where Thorsen takes her article and astutely observes how the kind of gaze Thorsen employs in fact moves the rural household very much into a place that is *à la mode* in the late 1980s.

Both Nevena Škrbić Alempijević and Silvy Chakkalakal begin their contributions in their student days. Significantly, the former writes from the perspective of her generation, the multiple expectations it faced in Croatia at the turn of the twenty-first century and the kind of disciplinary uncertainty it experienced "caught in-between theory and practice." Škrbić Alempijević captures the gap between the social, political and economic situation discussed

Regina F. Bendix 2017: She Grows Younger Every Year... Comment for the Anniversary Issue
Ethnologia Europaea 47:1, 84–87. © Museum Tusculanum Press.

in Konrad Köstlin's 1999 article, and the rise of new nationalism in the present – but she sees in Köstlin's analytic perspective tools that can be used for understanding also the rise or assertion of culture in resurfacing borders. Chakkalakal sketches what pulled her into the discipline in the first place: "Back then, my studies were clearly driven by a desire to understand my own positioning in the world." In that search, Kira Kosnick with her 2008 article on (post-)identities proved to be a lucid stab at scholarly classifications vis-à-vis lived realities. We are to glean that this view also represents maturing insights in turn valid for Chakkalakal – though no claim is made that they also stand for "her generation" or "the field," and this may indeed be uncertain in a present where diversity and assertiveness for divergent positionality and goals is not just a social but also a disciplinary reality.

Peter Jan Margry also situates his chosen article, Orvar Löfgren's "The Nationalization of Culture" from 1989, into dialogue with his professional biography. Thanks to a position at a research institute, Margry shifted or expanded from medieval history toward European ethnology. He recalls seeking to grasp what this field might be; he followed his new colleagues' suggestions to read *Ethnologia Europaea*, and found the first two decades of the journal disappointing, they "had lost the topicality of their time." Löfgren's article and the entire issue it framed, by contrast, broke out of such normal science; it catapulted the journal toward new questions to be looked at from new vantage posts.

Only Dorothy Noyes keeps her involvement with the field more veiled. Tasked with choosing a piece from the first decade of *Ethnologia Europaea*, she opts for two authors and places them within a yet larger comparative framework. Perhaps it was the dryness of Sigurd Erixon's first paper in the new journal whose founding he had worked for that made Noyes search for more fodder. At almost 80 years of age, Erixon died within a year of outlining, in the inaugural issue, what ought to be the unifying impulse for, as Noyes puts it, "a heterogeneous array of intellectual projects in Europe." He may have fought too many battles to have the stamina for an impassioned plea – and the very pragmatism of his mission statement may have contributed to the normal science Margry points to for the early decades of the journal. In Alberto Cirese's impassioned call for a true science that "has not only methods but clear goals and clear boundaries that permit the development of theory and a sector-specific perspective," Noyes found a protagonist who outlined a possible direction for the enterprise.

Through the coming decades, European ethnology could have been in fruitful cooperation with a number of transformative endeavors such as the "new directions in folklore" from the United States, published but a few years later, or the framework built by British cultural studies. That Cirese's plan remained rarely cited outside Italy is owed far more to the fact that his inaugural contribution was written in French than to his grounding in folklore and his Gramscian position – the latter has been circulated ever more in ethnographic fields once it was available in English. While Noyes elegantly brings Erixon and Cirese's papers into conversation also with a further one in German by Hermann Bausinger published in the second issue, one might have to admit that the one dimension where *Ethnologia Europaea* has struggled and shows signs of age is the realm of linguistic diversity among its target audience. As Orvar Löfgren points to in his final comment in this issue, *Ethnologia Europaea* has striven to address the linguistic as well as conceptual and institutional diversity in European Ethnology in different ways, again illustrating generational shifts and rejuvenation. After years of allowing for country portraits in the style of "in country X we practice ethnology in this manner," there followed initiatives bringing together ethnologists from different countries to address, jointly, a phenomenon or an important development. The journal found a way to leave behind the mold of a discipline practiced in various nations to the Europeanization of disciplinary approaches. And yet, the lingua franca English is spoken and *written* as a native tongue only in the one European country that voted in 2016 for Brexit (of course the Republic of Ireland also speaks and writes English, alas, not exclusively). Living in a Europe increasingly ravaged by populisms of the neo-nationalist sort, the language questions hover as uneasily as the question regarding ethnology's invariably socio-political position within this phase of what Löfgren calls De-Europeanization – invariably so, as our subject since its intellectual formation has always been entangled with state-making, from nation-building to the Europe of regions and back. Following Noyes sage reminder to "supplement the 'big tent' approach of inclusivity" with regular efforts to "rediscover the subterranean linkages between our external [disciplinary] linkages" would seem to be a crucial component of keeping *Ethnologia Europaea* on the path of regeneration.

Had I been asked to pick from *Ethnologia Europaea's* past a favorite issue, it would have been the one with the plastic flamingos on the cover. This surprising image announced, loudly and humorously, volume 35 (2005), entitled *Off the Edge* and edited by Orvar Löfgren and Richard Wilk. If ever an issue stood for breaking boundaries, rousing expectations, and inviting alternative ways of grasping everyday life ethnologically, it was this one. Inviting an array of authors to write about phenomena and practices that had so far not entered the ethnographer's mind, the editors created a platform for creativity and improvisation, surely among the most important and least discussed components of inventive scholarship. The flamingos were iconic for this move and they also provide opportunity to give some space to think about the covers which thus far go missing in this celebratory, intellectual assembly of contributions: they are worthy of inclusion and reflection. The flamingos inaugurated the journal's turn toward covers with evocative photographs, working with the stunning talents of Pernille Sys Hansen. Issue after issue she has managed to give the contents a particular spin, with montages, color screens, and enlargements; she whets the appetite of the reader, aesthetically arousing curiosity and interest in ever new contents. The flamingos and successive covers, always taking up an aspect of a given issue, were a significant move away from featuring the allegoric representation of Europe (by the Danish artist Nicolai Abildgaard from the late eighteenth century), uneasily seated on that bull, also known as Zeus, who did you-know-what with her. For some years, this image may have stood for what was an important component in *Ethnologia Europaea's* program: to remain dangling between standing for a responsible, grown-up discipline with ancient roots and being a flirtatious, young adult seeking a place for an ever-emergent discipline. The representation of the personified Europe, familiar from Greek mythology, anchored the idea of Europe in the distant past. The ancient sheen perhaps was meant to give the journal legitimacy and patina, reminding producers and readers alike that Europe had been imagined as a whole, a female body no less, before wars and ideologies created nation states. In hindsight and living in 2017, in a time where bullish leaders seek to break apart the hope to overcome the nationalism that is encoded in the European project, one sees additional reason for turning away from an image drawn from ancient civilization toward pulsating, colorful pictures drawn from everyday life. Before the allegorical Europe, there were many years during which a woodcut from Olaus Magnus' *Historia de Gentibus Septentrionalibus* from 1555 graced the cover. Showing peasants engaged in reaping corn, seemingly observed or commanded by another, elder and more richly clad actor, the choice of that image seems to still have been indebted to a European ethnology focused on the rural – though the contents of the journal were already far ahead of its external representation.

At least in the world of analog publishing, covers are the calling card of a journal. Judging by the fact that during my time as co-editor, it was the covers that my colleagues used to react to – often with joy – and not the content, we are called to attend to another reason for why supra-national disciplinary re-affirmation in both intellectual and strategic terms is a role that *Ethnologia Europaea* should continue to embrace assertively. A steady reader of the journal will observe that the journal has not just grown younger every year, the authors finding their way into the journal are no longer mostly the holders of professorships whose perspectives the journal makes internationally visible. Diversity in authors' age has been a crucial component of allowing *Ethnologia Europaea* to grow young topically while remaining sound academically. But openness to send young authors' work through the peer-review process is also part of editors' responsibility; in idealistic terms, editors promote younger scholars, acting as midwives to bring work to full fruition; in political terms, they assist those up and coming in the field to build the kind of curriculum vitae the neoliberal university expects. How to balance the intellectual and political roles scholarly journals invariably hold is one of the many editorial tasks – giving me reason to thank the current editors on behalf of all of us readers and to wish them stamina and many exciting and far-reaching article submissions to work with!

Regina F. Bendix teaches at the University of Göttingen since 2001. She is a native Swiss, studied and worked in the USA for a long time, and returned to Europe not least because the unifying of European nation states remains to her a crucial and exemplary movement for a politics distancing itself from nationalist populisms. *Ethnologia Europaea* is one endeavor serving this goal.
(rbendix@gwdg.de)

SIEF membership package

In December 2014 the membership of SIEF, the Société Internationale d'Ethnologie et de Folklore, voted in favour of making *Ethnologia Europaea* its official journal, after SIEF, the editors and the publisher of *Ethnologia Europaea,* Museum Tusculanum Press, had prepared the ground for a mutually agreeable association between organization and publication. SIEF was founded in 1964, *Ethnologia Europaea* in 1966, and as recent historiographic research makes quite evident, there was no love lost between the actors founding the two respective institutions. Some five decades later, it is safe to say that cooperation rather than particularization is the major coin of scholarship. Both partners share a profound interest in nurturing and promoting scientific research and communication within our field(s), in extending international collaboration among European ethnologists as well as in disseminating new ethnological knowledge to a wide readership.

Membership

SIEF gathers every two years for its international congress, where colleagues engage with one another's work and enjoy each other's company. The SIEF congress is an intellectual festival that showcases the state of the art in our fields and a ritual time in the academic calendar, crucial for building professional networks, a number of collaborative projects, finding inspiration, and cultivating friendships. Between congresses, SIEF's numerous working groups provide platforms for critical debate, networking, and exchange of information; they organize their own meetings and sponsor publications.

SIEF has two professional journals: *Ethnologia Europaea*, a printed subscription-based journal that all members receive by mail twice a year, and *Cultural Analysis*, an Open Access journal published online. In addition, SIEF communicates with members through its website and with two newsletters sent out every year.

The annual membership fee is € 35. Opting for a two-year membership in one go qualifies for a discounted price of € 67. Membership will support SIEF to grow as a strong professional organization, while allowing members to participate in the SIEF community and shape the future of the academic fields.

The membership package offers a great host of benefits, including a subscription to the lively and interdisciplinary, peer-reviewed journal *Ethnologia Europaea*. Members will receive printed copies of the biannual journal as well as electronic access to available backlist issues.

See more and apply for membership now at www.siefhome.org.